Goin

Catherine von Ruhland ~~mental issues for most o~~ with her local Friends ~~...~~ days, and began to explore the issues ~~raised~~ art and design. She undertook Environmental Studies as an option during a Librarianship degree course at Manchester Polytechnic (1982–85) and as Sabbatical Editor of the Student Union paper *Pulp* had it published on recycled paper.

After leaving Manchester Catherine continued to work as a journalist. She was previously Editorial Assistant at TEAR Fund and Press Officer for the Evangelical Alliance, and is Editorial Co-ordinator of the Christian Ecology Group's newsletter *Green Christians*.

Catherine von Ruhland

Going Green

Illustrated by Dan Donovan

Marshall Pickering
An imprint of HarperCollins *Publishers*

First published in Great Britain in 1991 by Marshall Pickering
Marshall Pickering is an imprint of
Collins Religious Division,
Part of HarperCollins Publishers
77–85 Fulham Palace Road, London W6 8JB

Copyright © 1991 by Catherine von Ruhland

Typeset by Medcalf Type Ltd, Bicester, Oxon
Printed and bound in Great Britain by
HarperCollins Manufacturing, Glasgow

Contents

'Pollution: it begins if you don't have the good fortune to have a mother who makes you pick up your orange peel and eggshells after a picnic. Whether it's in the Bois de Boulogne or on the beach at Saint Gildes.'

Simone Signoret, *Nostalgia isn't what it used to be*, Penguin, 1979, p. 405

To my parents, who first opened my eyes to God and the world around me.

1

Introduction

Pollution, famine, the Greenhouse Effect, the hole in the ozone layer. . . The world is in an environmental mess, and the problems we face can seem just too big for us to be able to do anything about them.

It's the easiest thing in the world to put our worries to one side and carry on living — fiddling while Rome burns. But shut off our consciences and do nothing and we become part of the problem rather than part of the solution. As Christians, God wants us to make an impact for Him, to be salt and light on this earth. That doesn't mean just looking out for other people, but caring about His planet too.

Of course we might not have much money and many of you reading this will not yet be old enough to vote, but you can still change the world in small but positive ways. Indeed, I've never been able to vote for the political party I've wanted to vote for in a General Election. But the things I choose to do in my everyday life and the lifestyle I live do make some small impact.

Both Christianity and Green thinking are very similar in this respect. Both believe that as an individual you can make a difference, that you are responsible for many parts of your life. This book is designed to help you think about the different areas of your life and how you can change each one to live more Greenly while walking God's way. Though this book is aimed primarily at people in their teens and twenties, I hope that others will find it prompts them to think about their lifestyles too.

It's true that there will be times when you feel that you're the only one living Greenly. You'll sometimes get

9

tired of having to explain why you live the way you do. Maybe you'll sometimes feel that few of your friends understand your concern for the world and the way we treat it. While reading this book, you'll soon realise that there are plenty of other Christians who care about God's earth and believe it's part of our responsibility as Jesus' ambassadors to help Him restore it.

There's certainly a lot to guide us in the Bible in both the Old and the New Testaments. And looking there, we find that living Greenly, living a life of self-sacrifice and acting as a steward of the world where we live, is entirely Christian.

It was only a few years ago that people who recycled and reused things were thought of as a bit obsessive, and a bit out of touch. Two or three years ago, people would tell me that I was born twenty years too late, that I should have been a hippy in the Sixties!

Now, being Green is very fashionable. It's more mainstream this time round and far more commercialised. These days you have to pay your way to show you're Green. The message is in the T-shirt, the cosmetics, the car that you drive. People seem to have forgotten the slogan that rose out of the title of Schumacher's book *Small is beautiful*[1] and the wisdom that went with it, suggesting that we put on the brakes and try and live in a manner which doesn't plunder the earth for its riches. For the world simply cannot cope with the pressure we put on it from the way we live.

And we have to realise that being a Green Christian can't be a passing fad. Jesus' words are true yesterday, today, forever. If being Green is a Christian response to the world's environmental difficulties, then we cannot change our colour. We must think about our lifestyles not just this year, but for the rest of our lives.

At the end of his book *The Mustard Seed Conspiracy*, Tom Sine tells of an elderly shepherd in southern France who, as his sheep grazed, sorted and planted seeds in the barren ground. Twenty years later, the old man was still alive and a natural forest now covered the once empty landscape.[2]. It's by doing little things now that change begins to happen. Out of little acorns, mighty oak trees grow.

Certainly, if we're strong, there's nothing wrong with making big gestures. A TV news story a good few years ago told of a suburban family who had a big sale of their house contents and gave the money to the Spastics Society. When asked what they were going to do now their house was empty, the woman of the house declared that they would replace the sold possessions with ones bought from secondhand and charity shops. What this family had done was a very drastic and radical action, but it was also a very simple idea. I don't know if the family were Christians, but their action did show the spirit of Christ.

Not that you have to clear out your home or bedroom in a similar gesture. For there are plenty of environmentally-friendly ways to make our lives less wasteful, and which suit the different levels of commitment different people are able to make. Many are outlined in this book.

Each chapter suggests practical ways of living which, in general, do not need a lot of money. You may well be still very dependent on your parents. They provide the roof over your head and buy the food you eat. They might still give you pocket money. Whether you live with your parents or not, if you're working your pay isn't likely to be high. And if you're a student you'll be pretty hard-up. But fortunately, money isn't everything when it comes to being Green and Christian.

What you do need is a good dose of initiative, imagination and creativity. These are the subtle talents God has given us which tend to be neglected as we become better off. Some people argue: why bake a cake, make an outfit, get your clothes second hand, go by public transport if you can afford not to? It's a fair question, but it suggests that doing such things is time-wasting and a trial, when all of them can be made interesting and rewarding.

These are values we should hold on to, and a good time to start doing so is now. For as people get older, many find themselves bogged down with career, home, family and financial responsibilities and their lives lose the spontaneity and enthusiasm of youth. They find it harder to appreciate the things that money can't buy and the sheer adventure and privilege of being alive.

Being Green and being a Christian help you hang on to valuing the wonders of God's world. Together they'll channel your zest for life, despite the awkwardness of adolescence, in very positive and fulfilling directions.

In his book *Who Switched The Price Tags*? Tony Campolo explains that when he asks adults what they'd really like to do with their lives, their eyes light up and full of enthusiasm they express exciting plans and ideas. And then he asks them why they don't go ahead and put them into practice, and their eyes turn grey and they find excuses and carry on living the way they've always lived. 'Right before my eyes they repress their dreams because they are afraid to take the risks.'[3]

As a teenager or young adult, you're at a stage in your life when so many things seem possible. You are a tremendous asset to the Christian Church and to the Green movement. You have few responsibilities and your sense of freedom means that while you're testing the waters of adulthood, you're often prepared to take risks or voice what others might see as outlandish opinions with a real conviction. You add spark.

Of course this isn't true for every adolescent. Some are weighed down with traumas and duties that adults would find it hard to deal with, others are unbearably shy or feel literally out of step with their developing bodies. Likewise many adults become less likely to take risks because they've got children, a mortgage, they're working their way up the career ladder . . . Not that that means that they can't go on loving life. Just that their priorities are different. They ain't got time any more.

And the thing about Christians and Greens is that their priorities are very different. Jesus turns our way of looking at the world upon its head. The last shall be first, the meek shall inherit the earth, turn the other cheek, love your enemy. The Greens say 'small is beautiful', 'act local, think global' and talk about limits to growth and a new economic system that isn't just based on producing and consuming more and more and more.

To the unbeliever and the untrained eye it can all seem so strange. They find it hard to understand that people are living a different way from what's considered normal and can be happy living without.

But this seemingly topsy-turvy way of looking at the world makes the ups and downs of life easier to deal with. Green and Christian values aren't based on putting your hope in material possessions. That will stand us in far better stead for the tough times. And these values are less likely to lead to disappointment as they centre on the basic enjoyable things about being human.

In his 'price tags' book, Tony Campolo tells of a group of old people who, looking back on their lives, told him what they regretted. One old man remarked, 'I wish I'd had more hot baths.'[4] Such a simple idea conjures up delightful images. The simpler the life, the less there will be to regret. It's a thought worth remembering.

God likes us to appreciate the simple things in life. After all, He does. The world is full of simple things that bring joy. And it is these things we most miss when they vanish. Many of them feature in the wide world around us.

Don't you love the sight of a blue sky full of great white fluffy clouds? I can remember as a young child standing in the middle of the school field and looking up at the sky imagining what it would be like to wander through their folds. Aren't you struck by a deep red sunset? Or the sound of heavy rain beating down when you're warm and dry inside your home? And the smell of the damp grass afterwards?

Use your senses. Listen to the sound of children playing at break, or the call of a blackbird on a summer's evening. Taste the warmth of home-made bread. Sit on a park bench and just watch the people walking past. Roll a pebble between your fingers. Smell the freshness of pine. (And you can now buy yourself a 'calorie-free' book packed with such scratch 'n' sniff delights as chocolate cake and lemon meringue pie! [5] Fun and delicious!)

I'm not saying that you should never enjoy what money can buy. Just that it doesn't buy everything and that you don't need it to enjoy God's world and feel a part of it. Of course it's nice to splash out on something we want occasionally, but funnily enough, when you can afford to indulge often, the enjoyment you once got from a possession soon wanes.

Paul McCartney tells a tale about John Lennon back in the sixties when they first became famous and had some money. John had always loved Jaffa Cakes and so went on a McVities spending spree. After a week of guzzling plenty of sponge, tangy orange filling and chocolate covering, he had had enough. He never wanted to see another Jaffa Cake ever again . . . That's a trivial example, but what about that top you almost broke the bank to buy two years ago which now you wouldn't be seen dead in?

Learn to appreciate the little things of life that are all around us. By looking at the world that way we end up caring better for the larger things. Look after the pennies and the pounds will look after themselves, goes the saying. The principle is the same.

If we make changes in our own lives, however small the impact on the world may seem, be assured that the knock-on effect will be large. God is a great one for lining up circumstances and coincidences to bring someone to Christ, to respond to someone in need, and yes, to restore parts of His creation. He values the contribution we can make as His representatives on earth. It is my hope that this book will inspire you to be bold in living a Green lifestyle for God.

2

Green Christians—
Off Colour?

To be Green these days is very fashionable. Everybody's claiming to be ozone-friendly, environmentally sound, and a pal of the planet. People, as the saying goes, are acting locally and thinking globally. But like any other political activity, it's important that there's a spiritual dimension, a change of heart, if real change is to take place. So where is God in all this?

The Christian way of looking at the environment has been largely ignored by the Green movement. Indeed, many Greens blame the Genesis model of mankind having dominion over the world as the reason for the mess we're in. Not that Greens only focus on the physical. They're looking for their own answers to what's happening to the earth, and how to respond.

James Lovelock developed the Gaia philosophy which ties in very nicely with the new environmental consciousness. The earth, he concluded, was a self-regulating organism. As someone has pointed out, this means that as the human race is the cause of so many of the world's problems, we could be self-regulated out of existence . . .

And though Lovelock could well argue that his theory has a scientific basis, it's promoted a Mother Earth fixation. Just hear actress Glenn 'Fatal Attraction' Close commenting on her interest in saving the world's rainforests: 'Our mother earth is dying. Perhaps a cure is possible but it will not happen unless we, her children can go beyond the short-sighted politics of self-interest and together, with ferocious determination, nurse her back to health.'[1]

Then along came the New Age movement. Remember the Age of Aquarius? That was all about Man as God moving into a New Consciousness, and becoming more loving, teaching the world to sing in perfect harmony. Being concerned about the environment was seen as just one aspect of humanity's new evolutionary step.

Certainly the anti-materialism at the base of Green philosophy attracts all kinds of spiritually-inclined people. And though for Christians that provides a far deeper starting point for discussion − I find you don't chat with Greens, you have hour-long conversations with complete strangers − it can be more difficult introducing them to Christ because they already have clear convictions about what they believe.

Green beginning

And where are all the Green Christians? And what do they have to say about the new interest in the environment? In fact, they're strongly maintaining that Green thinking has been around since God made the earth.

'In the beginning God created the heavens and the earth. . . Then God said, "Let us make man in our image, in our likeness, and let them rule over the fish of the sea and the birds of the air, over the livestock, over all the earth, and over all the creatures that move along the ground. . ." God saw all that he had made, and it was very good.'[2]

But since Adam and Eve ate from the tree of knowledge, we've tended to misinterpret God's words for our own ends, believing that it's okay to dominate the world and all its creatures instead of being stewards, caretakers of God's creation.

Guiding force

The Bible provides us with guidelines on how to use the

world's resources responsibly in a less than perfect world. The Old Testament with its directions for farming, looking after livestock and giving the land a rest is very similar to Green politics. The Green idea of our privilege in being responsible for future generations is matched by the Old Testament tale of family line and the impact of sin from generation to generation.

'God means his world to be managed by man, not exploited, and Christians ought to be among the first to raise their voices against all that would destroy rather than preserve the richness and the beauty of God's world — our home.'[3]

But we have ignored the Biblical model of *dominion* and instead chosen *domination* over all the earth, aiming ultimately to subdue it with our greed. Christianity is often criticised as being the reason for much of the damage that has occurred on the planet. But we should make clear to the critics that it is not our faith, but a combination of scientific theory and industrial progress among unbelievers and our own wrong understanding of God's Word that has brought about destruction.

We plunder the world's valuable minerals leaving a trail of devastation and pollution, we steamroller vast tracts of land for sprawling cities and industry to feed those cities, and we pour our waste into the mighty oceans and the atmosphere around and above us.

'This is God's creation that we are destroying: His gift to us that is being abused. He has made us stewards of this creation, and we ought to be asking His forgiveness of our corporate destruction and greed,' states John Biggs,[4] a notably environmentally-conscious President of the Baptist Union, during his one-year term of office.

Turning fear to hope
Our Green Christianity must involve an awareness of our corporate sin towards the planet and our own personal wrongdoings, and then a turning to God to apologise and

to ask His forgiveness. And it is here that Christianity offers hope to a crumbling world.

There is a lot of fear in the Green movement. A lot of its growth is the result of basic self-interest. People are frightened of the chemicals added to our food, of the rise in the globe's temperature, of time running out. The threat is personal and immediate.

The environmental crisis shows up sin for what it is. Without God, there is no way out. Practically every one of our actions in the developed West adds to the pressure on God's creation however Green we may try to be. Sure, your Green actions *do* make a difference because they slow down the rate of damage, but the UK economy, like other Western economies, is part of a system devoted to growth that the world just cannot take.

And so the knock-on effect of Green action has its minuses as well as its pluses. Take for example the idea of the electric car. It certainly *sounds* very Green – it doesn't pump out pollutants when it's travelling, it doesn't need petrol which is pumped out of the earth. But it has to be recharged regularly which means wiring it up to the electricity system. If coal-powered it produces sulphur dioxide into the atmosphere which mixes with the air to fall as acid rain, and if nuclear-powered it produces harmful radiation which causes leukaemia. It's the same with recycling. It's all very well to take your paper down to the paper bank, but a lot of it ends up as landfill rather than being recycled, or if recycled it adds printer's ink to our water system.

Without knowing God's power to make things happen with our small gestures, people can become very disheartened. Environmental destruction gets worse and worse and like sin ends in death. But Christians are motivated by God's hurt for His damaged world and the belief that God is ultimately in control. We know that at the end of time the earth will be restored and transformed.

Positively green

Contrary to what many unbelieving conservationists think, the basis of Christianity is truly for the careful treatment of the planet. It is therefore truly Green. As Philip Seddon explains: 'The Old Testament is literally the "earthing" of Christian faith. Genesis 1 precisely classifies the rhythms of the day and night, and spells out "categories of species and genera according to their kind."'

'Genesis 2,' he continues, 'makes very clear that man (adam) derives from the ground (adamah), and that human community is part and parcel of the animal world which God created. The Psalms perpetually praise God for creation. The theme of the New Testament (from Jesus' temptations to the vision of Revelation 21) is the re-creation of the world.'[5]

Until that time, the human race can never return to Eden. The world is tarnished by sin. So Christian Greens, while working for a better world, are well aware that it will not be complete before Christ returns. Perfection cannot be obtained in this world.

But if it's all going to be put right when Jesus returns, why bother trying to save the world now? So runs the argument of some Christians. Which is a bit like saying that somebody who's ill shouldn't go to hospital to be cured as they'll be perfectly healthy in Heaven.

Our presence on earth goes beyond helping to save human souls, for God has created all things, and each part of His world, though tainted by sin, reveals Him too. It's part of our Christian duty to work towards the world's re-creation.

'Two of Paul's greatest visions of renewed creation — Romans 8 and Colossians 1 — clearly connect God's act in Christ with both the human and the wider aspects of creation,' stresses Philip Seddon. 'The whole history of monasticism from St Anthony onwards, all nine centuries before St Francis, expounds the theme of the re-creation of Paradise.'[6]

We understand the Green slogan 'Act locally, think globally' from a Christian viewpoint. The Green's internationalist stance mirrors the Christian awareness of our interdependence with each other and with nature as part of God's marvellous plan for the world. And barriers of nationality crumble as we identify with other people across the planet.

Green living is often a gradual step-by-step approach which leaves deep imprints. As with Christianity, it's about ordinary people making choices in their day-to-day lives that make the difference: drinking a particular brand of coffee, washing with biodegradable soap untested on animals, finding uses for things one would otherwise throw away. Each one of us is of value to the global whole and to God.

Not ours to plunder
For Christian Greens, as with any Christian involved in politics, it's not just a case of choosing one philosophy over Christianity. Our politics should be about putting our Christian faith into action. Green politics, like Christianity, is very practical.

The similarities between the Green way of looking at the world and Biblical values shouldn't be ignored. When God placed us on this planet He didn't give it to us, as many believe, to use it for our own pleasure and greed. There is a pattern to its creation. The world remains God's while tainted by our feeble stewardship.

We have tended to look at the earth with the viewpoint that its minerals, its wildlife, the resources that it holds are simply here for our use. Even when we talk of good stewardship of God's world, our minds are still on what we can get out of it as long as we don't damage it too much, of course.

But when God put us here, it was with the instruction that we should look after it. But it was to look after it purely *for Him*. Creation doesn't have value because of

21

what we can get out of it. It has value because it belongs to God. 'We have no liberty to do what we like with our natural environment; it is not ours to treat as we please. Since we hold it in trust, we have to manage it responsibly and productively for the sake of our own and subsequent generations.'[7]

Too often, like a spoilt child grabbing a football and refusing to let anybody else touch it, we cry, 'It's mine!' A Green Christianity helps us get a glimpse of the way the world is meant to be. To help save the earth we first need to understand our relationship with the world and with God. Too often we fall into the trap of thinking that only by our own efforts will we preserve our global home. But by keeping it to ourselves we achieve nothing. It's only by knowing our place that we can truly give the planet back to Him.

ACTION STATION

- Read:

  Green Christianity: caring for the whole creation by Tim Cooper (Hodder & Stoughton, 1990).

  Green Finger of God by Maurice Sinclair (Paternoster, 1980).

  Caring for the Earth — the environment, Christians and the church by Keith Innes (Grove Ethical Studies no. 66, 1987).

  The Christian Green Heritage: world as creation by Edward Echlin (Grove Ethical Studies no. 74, 1989).

  Tending the Garden: essays on the Gospel and the earth edited by Wesley Granberg-Michaelson (Eerdamans, 1987).

- Be ready to speak of your Christian faith with Greens. Because Christianity has in the past had quite a bad press environment-wise, it's important that we put the record straight, and show others that Christians have plenty of good reasons to care for the earth.

- Recognise now that each one of us is responsible for a lot of environmental destruction. We can't not be. Pray for forgiveness and ask God to take your own Green actions and transform them so that they make a really positive impact.

3

A Different Way of Seeing Green

It's God who has prompted our interest in Green issues. Our faith in Him helps us see the world in a new light. His Holy Spirit opens our eyes to the injustices and evils of this world.

Some Christians are more concerned with people-based issues than with wider environmental issues. This is not necessarily a bad thing; we are all jigsaw pieces in God's puzzle for this world. But Green issues are interconnected. People are hurt by pollution. Living a Green lifestyle from a Christian perspective helps us to consider many of the issues that are important to God.

Friends in need
You may well have Green friends who are not Christians. Do pray for them. Being Green is about living a philosophy. Once we start living Greenly we find it makes its mark on every part of our lives. We see the waste all around us, we worry about the materials that we can't re-use or recycle. It's easy to become frustrated and depressed at how little seems to be done even though we're doing our best. There are times when we wish we didn't have a conscience and could be just as materialistic as everyone else!

But as Christians we can always turn to Christ and His example of the supreme sacrifice. He never promised us a rose garden when we gave our lives to Him. His path is narrow, and we carry our crosses as we follow in His footsteps. But we know His path leads to heaven. Our

24

non-Christian Green friends must face more doubt than we do about whether they're doing the right thing. Many people who put in long hours for the Green movement suffer from 'burn-out' and drift away.

When Jesus was facing a hard time He would leave His disciples and find a quiet place where He could talk with God. It is prayer that builds us up and prepares us for the road ahead. It calms us down, helps us put things in perspective and replenishes our spiritual resources. And Jesus Himself got to a point where He was tired, when He would rather not have to go through with the crucifixion. But His prayers alone at Gethsemane while His disciples slept drew Him close to God and gave Him the strength to follow God completely, certain that it was the best way.[1]

Green Jesus?

Was Jesus Green? Politicians of different parties have always liked to claim Jesus for their own. The truth is that Jesus is such a complete person that different aspects of His personality and the way He handled people lend themselves to different ways of looking at the world.

Animal rights followers certainly couldn't be happy with Jesus' apparent lack of concern for the Gadarene swine. When driving out demons from a man He pointed them to a herd of pigs which they promptly possessed and drove over a cliff to their deaths.[2]

But in this tale of a pathetic man made well, we also see the hierarchy of creation. Jesus is above the demons and has the power to punish them forever. But demons are quite able to torture a man and drag him screaming away from the presence of God. And Jesus sends the 'legion' among the pigs and so destroys a whole herd of animals. One man's soul seems to be worth far more than masses of swine.

Yet Jesus was well aware of the value of livestock to the people He lived among, and often used the image of sheep and lambs to reveal a truth to His followers. The Good Shepherd treats us in a way that provides a guide to how animals should be properly treated.

Jesus made the worth of every creature and plant that lives on the earth very clear. He told of sparrows that God watches over[3] and lilies of the field[4] which outstrip the beauty of anything we'll ever find in our wardrobes. But He stated that their relationship to Man was as a lower part of creation.

'Look at the birds of the air; they do not sow or reap or store away in barns, and yet your heavenly Father feeds them. Are you not much more valuable than they?'[5]

But this is in the context of our role as caretakers for Christ. It is because the plants and animals are 'lesser beings' that we should care for them, as a responsible adult watches over a child.

Creation story

God values creation for its own sake without man's intervention. The first five days of the six God spent completing His project were spent introducing the different 'layers' and distinctions of the world and the plants and creatures that lived there. And each day God liked what He saw and 'it was good'.

One gets the impression that He had a fabulous time painting the sky with stars and letting the air and water teem with living creatures. And this was before He got around to making us! On the sixth day God not only produced land-living creatures, but made man in His own image to complete and complement His creation. 'Thus the heavens and the earth were completed in all their vast array.'[6]

If you or a friend have a video recorder, or there's one your youth group can use, watch the Tear Fund video *Broken Image*.[7] Focusing on the poverty and people of the Philippines, it begins with a stunning creation story mime by Geoffrey Stephenson which is full of humorous

imagery and sheer fun. I have also heard Christian poet
Stewart Henderson recite a thrilling poem on the same
theme. It reminded me very much of Geoffrey's mime,
this time putting Genesis chapter one into modern-day
words.

But creation, God's perfect plan, was spoilt by
humanity's selfishness and desire to take control. And
with that step away from God, we lost the godly approach
to the rest of creation and the understanding of how it
was meant to be managed.

Man is out of step with the rest of the created order
and survival becomes a tale of pain, toil and struggle.[8]
And God banishes Adam and Eve from Eden, and then
locks the gate so to speak, so that they cannot return and
destroy it further. In one move, humanity is cut off both
from knowing God and from nature. And because we
were originally part of God's plan, destined to care for
creation, nature cannot be made whole without us.

A perfect world
But our hope is in Jesus Christ. He come not only to act
as a bond between us and God, but to bring the whole
of creation back to Him in one perfect peace.

> The wolf will live with the lamb,
> the leopard will lie down with the goat,
> the calf and the lion and the yearling together;
> and a little child will lead them.
> The cow will feed with the bear,
> their young will lie down together,
> and the lion will eat straw like the ox.
> The infant will play near the hole of the cobra,
> and the young child put his hand into the viper's nest.
> They will neither harm nor destroy
> on all my holy mountain,
> for the earth will be full of the knowledge of the Lord
> as the waters cover the sea.[9]

So, as Christians, our job is not just to bring people to Christ but to work towards rebuilding God's damaged empire. For God is not totally separate from the world. As its Creator, it is in a sense a part of Him, as a picture we paint or a story we write reveals a part of us. We have put something of ourselves into it. If something we have made is spoilt we are not hurt physically, but a tiny piece of our presence on earth has been affected. God Himself is not damaged by our selfishness. He is outside His creation in that sense. But He grieves for the dying, the lost and the lonely, and He is saddened by what is happening in His world. He has compassion for the suffering. And in that sense, part of Him is hurt too.

But the hurt of all that has ever been will one day be in the past. Here is where the hope of the Green Christian lies. The world will be renewed and made perfect just as we who believe in Jesus Christ will be made whole at the end of time.

And as Paul states so positively: 'I consider that our present sufferings are not worth comparing with the glory that will be revealed in us.'[10] What a thought! The oil spills, the global warming, the chemicals poured into the atmosphere, the extinction of vast numbers of species of plant and animal . . . All this pain and horror will be nothing compared with how it will look when God's put it all right.

Even without the pollution our lifestyles bring, even without a species being harmed, we are not seeing anything as it was meant to be. We're rightly amazed at the beauty of a peacock's plumage, and a crimson night sky. But we ain't seen nothing yet! God's promise is that the world will be returned to its former glory and will flourish forever.

'The creation waits in eager expectation for the Sons of God to be revealed. For the creation was subjected to frustration, not by its own choice, but by the will of the one who subjected it, in hope that the creation itself will be liberated from its bondage to decay and brought into the glorious freedom of the children of God.

'We know that the whole creation has been groaning as in the pains of childbirth right up to the present time. Not only so, but we ourselves, who have the first fruits of the Spirit, groan inwardly as we wait eagerly for our adoption as sons, the redemption of our bodies. For in this hope we are saved.'[11]

A Way Of Seeing

It's going to be a mind-blowing time. Artist Mark Boyle claims that as they grow older people put up shutters to the world around them. The world is so full of wondrous things, he says, that if we didn't we'd never do anything. We'd walk down the street, and at every leaf, twig, stone, colour, texture we'd stop and just go, 'Wow, amazing!' Scientists, even without God, have what they jokingly call the 'Fwor, lookadat' factor when they're stunned by something they see when peering down their microscopes.

Let's face it. The world's a pretty amazing place, and humanly speaking it is too much for us to take it all in. I do believe God shows us something more of what He has in store when we follow Him. We see the physical world in a new light. And it helps us to praise Him more. We can be satisfied just by looking with open eyes at the things we see around us. God makes us more sensitive to our surroundings and we smile and we sadden at what we experience. He gives us a heart for His world so that we can start helping Him rebuild it.

For knowing God's plan, we of all people should be prepared to get stuck in and help the environment withstand the pressures we heap upon it. And work to prevent many of them too.

Christians have often been blamed for environmental destruction. In fact, Christians by obeying God should be in the forefront of the Green movement. There's been enough destruction going on since the first sin. When we love Christ, God changes our hearts and minds so that we tread carefully on His world for Him.

ACTION STATION

- Read:

  The Mustard conspiracy by Tom Sine (MARC Europe, 1981).

  The Earth in Our Hands by Rowland Moss (IVP, 1982).

  A Christian Lifestyle by Horace Dammers (Hodder & Stoughton, 1986).

  Conservation and Lifestyle by Klaus Bockmuhl (Grove Booklet on Ethics no.20, 1977).

  Friends of the Earth Handbook edited by Jonathon Porritt (Macdonald Optima, 1987).

- Take time out. Look at the world around you, take in all you see slowly. Ask God to show you His love, His concern for this part of His world.

- Think of the Green things you do in your everyday life. Are they really the best way to help the planet? Are there better and more Green ways of doing things? Are there areas of your life which don't seem very Green at all? Think about changing them, and go ahead and do it.

- Are your Green acts specifically Christian? Use the references to the Bible mentioned in this book (the chapter and verse are given in the bibliography) to guide you. Check your Bible and read the neighbouring verses too. Pray that God will open your eyes to what He wants you to do.

4

Home Service

The idea that charity begins at home has been misunderstood over the years. Rather than a selfish excuse to look after 'number one' and your direct family, it's actually advice to look beyond the walls of your house.

Your home is a small image of the world. Resources are limited, relationships are important. When God gave Adam a companion Eve, not only was He creating the first human family, but He was showing how people must relate to the people around them so that they don't become lonely. If you care for your parents and brothers and sisters, if you are a helpful and loving member of your family or household, then you're learning how to deal with people outside your home in a godly manner. You're also sending out ripples of love that brighten the people around you so that they're better prepared to face the outside world.

In a Green sense, if you're charitable at home by taking care to use things resourcefully, buying fair-traded and environmentally safe products, then this 'charity' has an impact the world over. Reusing old envelopes might not seem such a big deal to you, but it says something to the person who receives it, and in a tiny way slows down the cutting down of the world's trees and conserves energy needed to make the paper.

A 'very old Chinese proverb' I saw hanging on the walls of a Henley guest house said something to me about the positive knock-on effect God brings to our lives and the world via our home life:

If there be righteousness in the heart, there will be beauty in the character,

If there is beauty in the character, there will be harmony in the home,

If there is harmony in the home, there will be order in the nation,

When there is order in each nation, there will be peace in the world.

We know that until Christ returns there will never be perfect peace and environmental destruction will continue. But as Christians living in the 1990s we must look closely at our personal lives to check that we reflect God in the way we treat our homes.

Home sweet home?

But firstly we must be sure that we regard our homes in the right way. Jesus said, 'Foxes have holes and birds of the air have nests, but the Son of Man has nowhere to lay His head.'[1] His disciples were nomadic too, travelling through towns and villages, and shaking the dust off their feet and going on their way if they weren't welcome.[2]

As Christians we must take up our cross daily and follow Christ − and we do not know where He will lead us. The Christian life is one of unattachment to worldly things and some Christians do indeed uproot and work in the far corners of the world.

But a lot of us live in more stable environments, so it's more a case of having the right attitude to our surroundings. God wants us to shake off our belongings so that we can serve Him all the better. We must be prepared to let go if that is what He wants. We mustn't put too much value on the decor, the size or the comfort of our own homes. It's what happens inside them that matters to God.

A one-room shack where His love glows through a family means as much as a mansion where the Christians who live there have flung open the doors for the community to enjoy it. In this sense we can take Jesus' words at face value. What's inside us we take with us wherever we go — so ultimately it doesn't matter where we live.

Nevertheless, our homes are a place to return to, a place where we've shared golden moments with family and friends. It's these glimpses of heaven that we tend to treasure in our hearts rather than the possessions we have. And that's a good thing.

'Do not store up for yourselves treasures on earth, where moth and rust destroy, and where thieves break in and steal. But store up for yourselves treasures in heaven, where moth and rust do not destroy, and where thieves do not break in and steal. For where your treasure is, there your heart will be also.'[3]

Think of the places where you've lived. What are the things you remember and value most about living there? Our most striking memories remain with us wherever we go. And even if they are not all good ones, it is important that we balance bad with good. Our memories of past experiences can colour the way we look at the world for the rest of our lives.

My parents still live in the house where I was born. I can walk into their bedroom and wonder that it was *there* that I made my entry into the world. When the sun shines through their cut glass door handles it scatters rainbows across the front room. As children, my brothers, sister and I would try and catch them in our cupped hands. And I treasure my childhood memory of my father carrying me from my bed one restless summer night and out into the garden to look at the stars.

I once watched a documentary about two young women who were born within the same week in the same nursing home and were accidentally swapped and given to the wrong mothers. The two families kept in touch and it all turned out happily in the end. But the most moving moment in the programme was when one of the young women explained what it had been like returning to her real mother's home having grown up as somebody else's daughter. As she heard the garden gate click behind her, she suddenly realised, 'That was the click I was meant to hear every day when I got home from school.'

It is these little things that matter to us and that touch our hearts, rather than the wall-to-wall carpet, three-piece suite and kitchen gadgets.

Open home

Reach out to your friends and open your doors and home. Maybe some of them aren't happy at home. The teenage years and those that follow on can be a time of disagreement between parents and their children. The generation gap is very real. It's not necessarily an age difference, but more a comparison of lives lived in different eras. How you live as a teenager in today's world is very different from how your parents lived when they were your age. But showing your friends that you appreciate what your parents do for you can help them see their own parents in a new light too.

A Christian home should be a haven away from the pressures of the world. Even if members of your household are unbelievers, don't let this put you off offering hospitality to others. Friendship is very valuable, and letting your home or your bedroom be a place where people you know can talk, play, and share their problems is putting God's love into action, and making good use of the space He's given you.

For a young person there's great pressure to go out with the crowd to discos, clubs, the pub. Your home can act as a cheap place of leisure. As you get older you find that just chatting with friends is good fun. Have a record evening, a clothes swap session. Dig out your old games – board games *can* be fun. Get friends to bring theirs along too so you don't get bored. One of the most humorous games, if you're in the right mood, is 'Twister'. It's designed for young children, but even young adults get a laugh out of the contortions you find yourself in by putting your left hand on a red circle, right foot on a blue circle . . . My own set did a vanishing act. I have a feeling that it ended up at a student party.

You may be too young to remember the power cuts of the 1972 Winter of Discontent. It must have been a bit trying for adults, going to work in the dark, buying candles, just not being able to use the 'lecky'. But for children it was an exciting time — having baths and going up to bed, doing jigsaws, playing games, all by candle-light. And having to do without the TV, record player, and finding something else to do for a change.

Why not stage a Powercut Party? Get plenty of candles in, make up some nibbles and sarnies and find a mirror or two to reflect the light. Turn off all electrical appliances and have an evening of enjoying each other's company without having to use artificial sound to banish silence. Make your own music, or take time to *listen* to what people have to say.

Open your home to God, too. The house or flat where you live might not be very big, but be sure to find a small corner where you can be alone with Him regularly. It can be difficult if you share a room with a brother or sister or flatmate, particularly if they're not Christians. If you prefer to pray and read your Bible at night, it's here that the ol' 'torch under the bedclothes reading a book' routine comes in handy. Or kneel at your bedside and pray in the dark instead. And remember that however small your quiet space, God is there. With prayer, a cell is transformed into a chapel.

Home is where the art is
The way you decorate the place you live says a lot about the person you are. There's a good chance that if you live with your parents, it's they who help you decide the colour scheme of your bedroom. But as you get older, they should give you greater freedom to make your own

choices. Even if you live away from your parents, it doesn't necessarily mean that you can do what you like with your living space. Though I do know someone who as an art student painted her whole room black, and another living in a hall of residence who covered his walls in silver foil.

What you can do is pin up pictures and add things to cover up the neat stuff. My sister nailed a piece of wooden garden trellis onto the wall and she hangs jewellery, clothes, photos, holiday mementos and gig tickets from it. This doesn't damage the wall paper behind.

And you don't need lots of cash to make your place your own. Now's the time to put to use God's gifts of imagination, creativity and initiative. Pictures can be ripped from magazines, posters can be collected from record shops before they're thrown away. At my parents' home, a cardboard Cliff sprawled on his bed hangs above my bed. Where I live at the moment I've Paul McCartney playing his guitar on my mantelpiece. Both cut-outs were free and kindly reserved for me by record dealers. Art exhibitions, particularly photographic ones often have good publicity posters. Some will be on sale, but others – if you ask nicely – will be handed over.

I wouldn't advise ripping pics of your favourite star from billboards. But I admire the ingenuity of my mate Joe who while studying in Manchester would, after a heavy rainfall (and it rains a lot in Manchester), leave his room to nip across the road to the row of boarded-up shops and gently peel off the soaked posters – their gum washed away – from the hoardings.

Postcards fill walls as well. When I've lived in places with white walls or brick, I've covered the bareness with pics of all shapes and sizes so there's hardly a spot of the background to be seen. It brightens up a place.

Chances are, over the years you've been on holiday and picked up shells and pebbles. These make great ornaments and help us appreciate the beauty, the texture and the life of God's creation. If like me you're not very green-fingered, get a tough plant — a spider plant, a cactus — that you can watch grow, but which takes little care. Cacti, maybe because of their shape and solidity, seem to take on characters of their own. For years we had one called Long Bill which grew taller and taller until, unable to hold its own weight and increasingly aging around the middle, it toppled over. But as it lay dying, it still grew. Five or six little cacti budded from its now horizontal body, each of them nourished on the flesh of Bill. New life sprouted from the old, and we accepted that although Long Bill was broken, this was the natural cycle in its desert habitat.

Ordinary everyday objects can look great on a shelf and often have a story to tell. The famous Coke bottle is a design classic, its shape based on that of the coca pod. Wandering around the Kenyan town of Eldoret, I came across a row of workshops where pots and pans are made from old cans and professionally welded. The only giveaway of their humble origin is the lettering on the sides. I bought a well-crafted metal funnel for myself and it hangs on my wall to show off the skill of the metalworker.

Plenty of shops sell ornaments and decorations that are pretty tasteless and totally useless except for the purpose of sitting on a shelf and trying to look pretty. I call these shops 'junk shops'. I'm not saying that we shouldn't buy ornaments to make our rooms look attractive. (I have a thing about penguins and have accumulated quite a few ceramic ones, my friend Julia prefers pigs . . .) But we should think for a start about whether we really need them. And we can check out antique stores and charity shops for pieces from the past. And we can be sure to look for the beauty, the shape and the unusual to celebrate in the ordinary and everyday.

Green house

We can all dream about the house where we would like to live. But wherever we find we live, God wants us to use our homes for His glory. It's about using the limited resources of our homes — space, number of rooms, whether there's a garden or not — to touch the wider world.

Housewives are some of the Greenest people around. Through the necessity of balancing the housekeeping budget, they tend to be experts at reuse, recycling and restoring without even realising it.

If you want to influence your family in a more Green manner, then start by encouraging what's already being done. Old sheets converted into pillow cases, fruit and vegetable peelings put on the compost pile or boiled up for soups, and even baking cakes and pies can all be seen in a Green light. Families pass furniture, ornaments and even good quality clothes and shoes down through the generations.

But what of the excess that can't be reused within the home — bottles, boxes, cans and plastics? Ideally, glass bottles and jars should be reusable or returnable. Jam jars are ideal for holding nuts and dried fruit, and household bits and pieces, make-up, pens. Make them into colourful ornaments by filling full of brightly coloured marbles or wooden beads. On my mantelpiece — alongside Paul MCartney! — I have an arrangement of a tall green wine bottle, a hexagonal jam jar acting as a small vase and a collection of brown glass pill and Marmite bottles of different sizes. Light shining through the glass casts interesting shapes on the white wall behind.

Milk bottles are a very Green idea. Do encourage your parents or flatmates to use the doorstep delivery system — not just because it's an excellent service, but because there's also a tremendous saving in resources. Milk floats run on electricity, and individual milk bottles are used over and over again. If your household drinks fresh orange juice, try and make sure they get it either straight from the fruit or out of a milk bottle from the milkman. The wasteful alternative is to buy from your local grocers which involves the higher cost of transporting the orange juice, and the problem of disposing of a waxed cardboard container that can only be used once and won't decompose.

Take other bottles to your local bottle bank – and if nobody in your household is bothered, make it your duty to make the effort yourself. Contact your local Council or branch of Friends of the Earth to find your nearest collection point.

Better still, make sure the fizzy drink you drink comes in a returnable bottle. Some brands of fizzyade including Corona and Tizer still come in deposit bottles. Just rinse and return to the shop you got them from.

Either way, choose to buy drinks in bottles rather than in cans as glass made from sand made from stones and shells is basically renewable. The raw materials for cans – aluminium and tin – must be dug from out of the earth. But if you do use cans, not only should you take them to your local can bank, but you can collect the ring pulls too. These can be sent to the British Kidney Patients Association to help buy kidney machines. Most unwanted household items have some charitable use. Aluminium foil can be taken to Oxfam or sent off to the Guide Dogs for the Blind appeal.

It always seems a waste to throw away good cardboard boxes and plastic cartons. If you've a younger brother or sister who goes to primary school or if you know someone in your street who does, ask them to take your spare boxes to their school for modelmaking. Egg cartons can go, too, though if your local greengrocer or market stallholder sells eggs from an egg tray, they'll be pleased to have your boxes.

A couple of plastic bottles are useful in the house if you want to go on picnics as you can fill them with diluted

orange or lemon juice for refreshment. Large PET bottles
— those massive ones with the black bottoms which
bounce when you drop them — are recyclable though at
the moment it's difficult to find places to get them
recycled. Plastic bags are always welcomed at the less
upmarket secondhand shops (take one when you go
shopping so you don't need another), as are coat hangers.

As we become more concerned about the world's
resources, we find ourselves searching for ways to use
them carefully. God opens our eyes to the potential of
the world He's created, and shows us how to share its
wealth carefully.

Reuse is far better than recycling. It's energy-saving
and there's not so much pollution involved. Do take your
newspapers to your local paper bank, but remember
that's not the best use for them. Newspaper is useful as
a bedding for pets, as compost, to line bins, and more.

When we're good stewards of the things we use in our
daily life, it has a knock-on effect on our finances, too.
The money saved can be sent to a charity or given to your
church. When we start re-using envelopes we find that
we no longer need to buy them. Use scrap paper instead
of gummed labels and you save money there, too. Your
faraway friends see your letters coming! Whenever you're
about to throw out sheets of A4 paper, check to see if
only half the page is used. Tear the plain pieces off and
use for letter writing.

Whatever comes into your possession, have a clear idea
of where any waste is going to end up. Very little should
go in the bin. One landlady actually thought me rather
eccentric because, as she complained, 'You never have
any rubbish.' But then she chucked me out of her place
because with all the paper I *did* have, she thought I was
a fire hazard! Ah, well.

But it's true. You do need some space, a collection
point in your home where you can store the materials to
take to be recycled. And you need space for your paper

and envelopes, and time to sort your materials and take them away.

That's not necessarily a bad thing. It gives us space to look at our homes anew, to value them as our parents' or landlord/lady's places and accept their ownership in a similar way to how we see God's ownership of our lives and our planet. Our homes are small versions of the wider world. How we treat them makes a great impact on the planet.

ACTION STATION

- Read:

  Home Ecology: making your world a better place by Karen Christensen (Arlington, 1989).

  The Human Home: the myth of the sacred environment by J.A. Walter (Kingsway, 1985).

  Design and Decorate Your Room by Felicity Everett and Paula Woods (Usbourne, 1989).

- Have a blitz on your possessions. Sort out what you can and can't do without, and give the things you no longer want or need to friends or to charity shops and jumble sales.

- Reduce pressure on the world's resources by sharing what you own with the people with whom you share your home.

- If your council doesn't provide paper and bottle banks, write to the environmental officer and ask that they be provided in your streets.

- If you've room for a pet, avoid the exotic creatures that have been transported from faraway lands. Contact your local branch of the RSPCA or PDSA or your neighbourhood vet to see if they know of any strays or unwanted animals that need a home.

5

Food for Thought

Food is more than fuel for our bodies. What we eat can make the difference between feeling healthy or sick, sluggish or alert — and it can touch our consciences too. If, as Paul declares, our bodies are the temple of the Holy Spirit,[1] we should be careful that what we eat isn't bad for our physical and mental health. But we must also look beyond ourselves and think of how our pattern of eating damages the land and the people who work and live on it. And how it affects our relationship with God.

Take a humble cup of tea or coffee. Certainly refreshing, and tea in particular is such a British institution that we don't give much thought to where it came from. But as with other 'cash crops', large areas of good land in the Third World are used to grow it and the local people who work on it for meagre wages are left with the poor soil for growing their own food to feed the family. Because the poor soil doesn't contain the nutrients plants need to thrive, often the harvest is small and people go hungry.

It is this sort of thing that we need to make the effort to know about. We can encourage parents or determine ourselves to buy alternatives like Tear Fund tea or Traidcraft coffee from a church, or Nicaraguan and African coffee from the local Oxfam shop. This tea and coffee is grown by small Third Would communities and most of the money raised goes directly to the people who grow it so that they're able to improve their lives.

When Jesus declared to the Devil that man cannot live by bread alone,[2] he stressed the need for spiritual sustenance, too. If we are to care for God's creation, then we must put the food on our plates and the drink we drink under the microscope of our faith.

Too many cooks?

Chances are, if you live with your parents it will be they who feed and water you. And even amid all the talk of the coming of the 'New Man', in most families it's still Mum who cooks. In many homes, the person who cooks can feel left out of family life. While they're stuck in the kitchen 'slaving over a hot stove' everybody else is watching TV, sitting outside in the sun or chatting in the front room. Maybe the reason women tend to get together in the kitchen whenever the extended family meets is that they've been there themselves on their own and know the feelings of isolation.

Yet this shouldn't be so. The kitchen should be the centre of a household where everyone enjoys a chat, helps with the spud peeling and feels part of the family. But though this might seem the case in glossy Sunday supplements and in 'Mother makes five' type sitcoms, in reality a lot of family kitchens are just too small to squeeze everyone in. If you don't cook yourself, why not make an effort to join the household cook in the kitchen?

Cooking and cleaning up afterwards can be a bit of a chore if someone has to do it every day. Why not help out, and try some cooking yourself at least once a week and give the household chef a break?

Don't tell yourself you can't cook. Cooking is like dressmaking or DIY. All you need is to be able to read so that you can follow the instructions. Maybe you had domestic science lessons at school but still feel pretty hopeless. So did I. I used to spend all my lessons looking for a left-handed potato peeler.

But since I've left school I've found that I thoroughly enjoy cooking and baking food. I make my own soups, cereals, sauces and salad dressings as well as main courses — and have yet to find anybody who doesn't like my

Danish Apple Pudding! Cooking is thoroughly creative and fun. When did you last have a good excuse to muck around with dough, make shapes with pastry, and get clarted up with flour?

Once you've got stuck in, there's time to stop awhile and think and pray. Mixing marg and flour between your fingertips to make pastry not only mirrors the mulling over in your mind which you're able to do in the process, but also helps you get right to the roots of the food you'll eventually eat. I find it's much easier to thank God for my food when I've felt part of the production process. When I use natural ingredients instead of getting it all out of a packet, I value more the sun and rain bearing down on the crops, the health of the soil, the work of the farmers and the transport of the ingredients to my local health food store or greengrocers.

Food for free
Wholefood, people argue, is far more expensive than ordinary stuff. But prices are coming down as health food is no longer just sold in health food stores, so that excuse is less of an excuse these days. What's more, because a lot of good food like fruit and veg doesn't have to be bought packaged, you can actually get it very cheap from conventional markets and greengrocers.

When you buy food from these sorts of places, you soon realise that it doesn't have to be unblemished for it to taste nice. Just because an apple isn't polished and rosy red — like something straight out of Walt Disney — doesn't mean it's not an apple. It's a good idea to give your fruit and veg a good wash and scrub before you bite into it to reduce the risk from chemicals. But otherwise remember that bruises are nothing more than bruises. Mud is just part of the outer layer that can be washed off. We learn to see the value of the fruit or vegetable beneath.

And when you're on your travels taking short cuts through parks and green spaces and wandering along alleyways, you begin to appreciate the food that's there for the taking. Brambles, bilberries and apples make fine jams, summer puddings and wine or are great eaten on the trot and shared among friends.

A ramble with my brother Chris is fascinating as he spies and identifies mushrooms, and picks them and fries them at home later. He's read Richard Mabey's *Food for Free*[3] and you should too before picking wild mushrooms. It's a highly inspiring book that shows you what you can and can't eat from the wild in this country. As Maybey admits, 'It is the intimacy with wild things that foraging can bring that seems to be most richly enjoyed. I can say this with some feeling myself, being less of an intensive gatherer these days than a devotee of the wayside nibble.'

When Jesus and his disciples nibbled corn at the side of a field, they weren't just redefining God's law about what to do on the Sabbath, but showing that eating 'on the hoof' from the fruits of the countryside is perfectly acceptable. In those days, farmers left a part of their crop specifically for the poor to eat. Foraging in the open air on a hot summer's day helps us enjoy the taste and abundance of the food God has given us.

Eating out

For most people eating out means going to a cafe or restaurant. Though I once saw a painting of three kids sitting on the pavement munching chips out of newspaper given the same title.

The multi-racial nature of our cities means that people have a world of menus from which to choose. If you take a bus through Rusholme, Manchester's Asian district, you'll see curry houses with windows piled high with brightly coloured Indian sweets. In London's Soho, well known for its meals from the Orient, even the street names are in Chinese.

Take advantage of the world of tastes and delicacies

on your doorstep and experiment with the flavours of different nations. And don't dismiss certain foods — pizzas, tacos, even fish and chips — as boring just because you eat them as fast food. Cooked properly and with care, they taste so much better than the takeaway 'plastic' versions.

On the face of it, fast food is certainly convenient. You feel hungry when you're out with friends, you pop into your local takeaway, order french fries, a double-decker burger and a creamy shake, and before you've taken a bite you're on your way. Fast food is suited to our high-speed modern lifestyles, but it leaves pollution and destruction in its wake.

All fast food comes wrapped, but because it's designed to be eaten quickly, the plastic and cardboard containers are just thrown away. Not only is this an eyesore, but it attracts vermin after the scraps of food, it adds money to the cost of your food and it uses up valuable resources for a very limited reason. Fast food is as 'convenient' as products in our throw-away society are 'disposable'. Neither is true.

Try to avoid using fast food restaurants. If you and your friends want to meet for a cheap bite go to an old style 'caff' where drinks are served in proper cups and glasses, and plates and cutlery are washed up instead of being thrown away. There's often a much better down-to-earth atmosphere, even though it's shabbier than the gleaming fast food palace further along the street.

The catering trade isn't known for its good pay or conditions. George Orwell's *Down and Out in London and Paris* is enough to put you off ever eating in a French restaurant again. Some chains of eating places are known for the poor way they treat their staff. That's something to bear in mind as much as the way your food's been treated. Instead of eating out as often as you do now, why not invite your friends around for a bite or a 'bring and share' meal instead which works out much cheaper and can be much more fun. And you don't have to kill the fatted calf. A huge bowl of pasta, some sauce, a bowl of salad and fresh, warm bread never fail to please. Rather than running up a huge supermarket bill to entertain your close friends, set yourself the challenge of cooking them a meal from whatever is in your fridge and food cupboard at the time.

Meat is murder?

I've had 'vegetarianism isn't biblical' thrown at me in my time, and MP John Gummer declared that if God didn't want us to eat meat He would have given us more than one stomach. But in fact vegetarianism was very much part of life in the Garden of Eden before the Fall.

'Then God said, "I give you every seed-bearing plant on the face of the whole earth and every tree that has fruit with seed in it. They will be yours for food. And to all the beasts of the earth and all the creatures that move on the ground − everything that has the breath of life in it − I give every green plant for food." And it was so.'[4]

But after the Fall the world was turned on its head. Following the Flood, God told Noah of a new order. 'The fear and dread of you will fall upon all the beasts of the earth and all the birds of the air, upon every creature that moves along the ground, and upon all the fish of the sea; they are given into your hands. Everything that lives and moves will be food for you. Just as I gave you the green plants, I now give you everything.'[5]

As a Christian, it is not wrong to eat meat. But increasingly Christians are questioning the morality of eating flesh when health is at risk, people are starving, animals are treated appallingly and rainforests are felled. All these are by-products of the meat market.

I became a vegetarian in my late teens. I was increasingly involved in the animal rights movement — it was the early 1980s and the era of the big demo — and it got to the point where it just seemed hypocritical to eat meat. I bought a copy of Janet Hunt's *A Vegetarian in the Family*[6] which has served me well ever since, and I made the switchover from meat to veg on holiday, so that by the time my family returned home my mother was used to the idea!

Other Christians are worried about the amount of chemicals and hormones pumped into animals during the farming process. Their concern is fair enough. In Puerto Rico where the traditional diet is chicken, girls as young as five were reaching puberty and young boys developed breasts because a local factory was injecting the female hormone oestrogen into the poultry to help it grow.

The mass production of meat and dairy products forces God's animals into the living hell of factory farm conditions. Chickens are cooped up in minute cages, calves are taken from their mothers and shut up in darkened sheds so their white flesh can be sold as veal, and intelligent creatures like pigs live in small stalls in which they can't turn round.

Not only that, but they are fed grain that could be used to feed people. And even when animals are given plenty of space to roam they can threaten the landscape. Beef cattle bred for hamburgers in Central America have led directly to the destruction of the rainforests as land is flattened to let the animals roam.

Clearly vegetarianism is worth considering in the light of this information. But many people today eat far less red meat than they used to. Think about how much meat you eat and see if there are any times when you can cut down. Or why not make a vegetarian meal for your family?

The food we eat must be looked at in the light of our Christian faith. Today, it is no longer a local issue with local solutions. Our meals are made from ingredients from across the world. What we eat literally has far-reaching consequences.

ACTION STATION

- Read:
  The Politics of Food by Geoffrey Cannon
  (Century Hutchinson, 1987).
  Christianity and the Rights of Animals by
  Andrew Linzey (SPCK, 1987).
  *Compassion, the Ultimate Ethic. An
  Explanation of Hunger* by Victoria Moran
  (Thorsons, 1985).
- Get yourself a good, basic cookery book and
  work your way through it. When you reach
  the end, begin all over again only this time
  just using the recipes of foods you enjoyed.
- Have a baking day when you prepare and make
  the food for the meals you're going to eat over
  the next six days to save money, time and
  energy.
- If you're a vegetarian, don't be dogmatic about
  it. When you're at a friend's or relative's
  home and they serve you meat because they
  don't know you're a veggie, don't cause a
  scene. They've taken the time and trouble to
  feed you, and chances are any unwanted meat
  left on a plate will end up in the bin anyway.
  That's no kinder to the animal which was
  killed.
- Have a day of fasting to clear out your system,
  focus on God and identify in some small way
  with the world's hungry. Give the money you
  save to a charity working to reduce poverty.
- Eat only health foods and avoid white bread and
  white sugar and other foods where all the
  goodness has been removed. You'll feel better
  for it and more ready to serve God.

6

Dress Sense

There is tremendous pressure to look fashionable. Pop
pin-ups, glossy fashion spreads, the way people dress in
the movies, shop window displays, and friends all have
an influence on the choices we make about the clothes
we wear.

But if we are fashion-conscious, we need to be careful.
Sure, God helps us appreciate the shape of an outfit, its
bright or subtle tones, and the way it suits the wearer just
as He helps us enjoy the landscape He created. In a multi-
cultural society, too, it's a delight to people-watch and
absorb the view of the rich variety of clothing from across
the world which enhances our own city scenes.

And often fashion designs are influenced by God's
creation. Fashion seasons of fresh spring prints, bold
summer patterns, glorious autumnal hues and heavy
winter wear mirror the turning of the globe. It's no accident
either that established British styles are warm and earthy
tweeds, and that Scandinavian fashion works best in basic
greys, blacks and browns highlighted by vivid flashes of
pink, lilacs and golds — thrilling like an Arctic sky.

But God does not want us to be over-concerned about
something as fleeting as fashion; there is no need to worry
about what clothes we are going to wear. They are not
as important as the fashion industry likes to suppose.

'Consider how the lilies grow. They do not labour or
spin. Yet I tell you, not even Solomon in all his splendour
was dressed like one of these. If that is how God clothes
the grass of the field, which is here today, and tomorrow
is thrown into the fire, how much more will he clothe
you, O you of little faith!'[1]

Which means that we don't go on a rash spending spree as soon as there's money in our pockets. If God wants us to look after His world for Him, then He doesn't want us craving after the latest outfit, satisfying our fashion desires only to crave after the next 'latest fashion' in a month's time − and wasting the world's resources and polluting the environment in the manufacture and disposal of our clothes as we go.

'If one were to carry the ecological arguments to their logical extreme,' cautions Jonathon Holliman, 'we would all be wearing uniforms, durably constructed from the least-polluting and most readily washable material. Clearly this is not reasonable. But if you carry clothing design to the other extreme, you have the fashion industry. Buying a wardrobe that becomes obsolete in a year is clearly not very reasonable either.'[2]

Ronald Sider in his 1977 classic *Rich Christians in an Age of Hunger*[3] suggests that Christians attempting to live a more simple life refuse to keep up with clothing fashions. Virtually nobody, he claims, need buy any clothes, except perhaps shoes, for at least two to three years. There seems no reason why that claim shouldn't hold true today. Does that sound impossible? Let's take a look.

It's certainly a challenge, but God has provided us with subtle and useful mental skills such as imagination, initiative and creativity with which we can approach the clothes we already own, and which we can use when we go shopping. As He changes our hearts and minds He helps us to be more satisfied with less. He shapes our tastes and the way we view ourselves so that we come to learn the styles that best suit us and can stand firm against the quick-change world of fashion.

Uniformity

Take school uniforms. Now, they're designed to iron out wealth and class differences between the pupils. If everybody looks the same, the theory goes, background won't be a barrier to friendship. But you've probably noticed that despite the similarity of each individual's uniform, there are fashions in the way people tie their ties, arrange the badges on blazer lapels, wear their hair, vary their shoe styles, and so on.

Within the restrictions laid down by the uniform, students still manage to find small ways of adapting their outfit into a more individual style. A white blouse or shirt, for example, can be worn buttoned up, half-buttoned, over a T-shirt, knotted at the waist. . . and by experimenting and learning to adapt such a basic item of clothing, you begin to see possibilities available in your out-of-school wear, too. During the Punk movement and its aftermath, singers including Sting and Bob Geldof dug out their old school ties and wore them slung loosely over their dishevelled and torn shirts . . .

Uniforms are resource-saving. Whether at school, working in a Saturday job or employed full-time in a post where uniforms are compulsory, they mean that you won't need so many clothes yourself and won't ruin or wear out your favourite ones. If you don't have to wear uniform, then it's an idea to wear fairly basic but smart styles that can be dressed up with jewellery or a bright jersey and worn regularly in different ways instead of spoiling your best clothes. When clothes you originally bought to wear outside your workplace, perhaps for a special occasion, begin to lose their 'specialness', then switch to dressing in them for school and work.

God doesn't necessarily want us all to look alike, though it's not unusual for members of Christian communities to wear the same outfits. Although God focuses on our hearts to see the true person beneath the skin, He has make us creative beings. To use these skills in a careful and resourceful way to adapt or embellish a piece of clothing extends His Kingdom.

Make do and mend

Although very much a war-time phrase used by your grandparents at a time of shortages and rationing, 'make do and mend' remains relevant today. It sounds a bit desperate that you should have to rely on the possessions you already have, but there's a lot of fun involved.

By changing buttons, lengths of skirts, widths of trouser legs, you can create original and interesting clothes. If you know how to sew, embroider or knit you can adapt and recreate your entire wardrobe. And don't regard these skills as 'just for the girls' as a lot of boys — and men — do. Kaffe Fassett (a man!) has revolution-ised the way knitters think about pattern through his hand-knitted designs. If you've an old jersey, then you could unpick it, wrap the wrinkly wool around a hot water bottle to straighten it out and reknit it into a wild-patterned sweater. Combine the craft of knitting with animal conservation, and make yourself a striking jumper featuring an endangered beast. Royalties from the *Knitting Wildlife* book of patterns[4] go to the World Wide Fund for Nature.

Dyes are useful, too, though potentially very messy, for brightening up any tired clothes and for coordinating the colours in your wardrobe. And there's more to it than hippyish-looking tie-dye and batik, though even these techniques can look very up-to-the-minute. Go for a straight one-colour cold-dye or use dye-pens to 'graffiti' plimsolls, old school shirts and white lab-coats.

Haberdashery stores or market stalls are great places to find bright buttons, dyes and remnants of exotic materials for altering your clothes. Try the local furnishing department and charity shops and check your family's cast-offs for accessories and outfit ideas, too. Don't despise the humble jumble sale either. A spending spree there will set you back a pound or two and you'll come away with armfuls of stuff for half the price of a card of buttons at London's Covent Garden.

And when you're spending time in all this re-creating, ask yourself how you feel about doing it. You'll notice how exciting it can be to see ideas for action developing into practical activity. Look at people around you, flick through magazines for ideas — and determine that you can look as good for a fraction of the price. Maybe you've an old pair of jeans that could be cut down into a great pair of shorts, or a jacket that could be shortened to a more boxy style.

An item once gathering dust at the bottom of a drawer in readiness to be thrown out gains new possibilities. You'll begin to see the potential in everyday objects which people throw away. And as an ambassador of Christ on this earth, you're seeing as God sees and helping to re-create His world from out of the dust of the Fall.

Dressed to kill
Leather looks good, but it had a previous owner. While there seems to be no healthy alternative to wearing leather shoes — though you can get away with flip-flops and rope-soled espadrilles in the summer — personally, as a vegetarian, I try to avoid wearing it for any other reason. You can argue that as most leather is a product of the meat-market, the skin's available anyway, and if you do eat meat there's no reason not to wear it, though avoid the snake and alligator skins.

It's no guarantee that just because you pay more at an upmarket chain store your shoes are going to last any longer than a cheap pair bought at a downmarket one. Either only buy them in the sales or go to one of those more select shops like the Natural Shoe Store, Anello & Davide or Church's, and treat yourself to a pair that if treated with respect will last for years. Polish your shoes and make use of shoe repairers to make your footwear last as long as possible.

But what about fur? Isn't that the same? Unfortunately not. The Inuit of the Arctic slaughtered seals for their meat and fur which combined with fishing enabled the communities to be self-sufficient. They were careful not to overfish or overkill the seals because then they themselves would die. This is the type of care God wants us to take over His creation. We must keep a balance between giving and taking.

But wearing fur grew in popularity and became highly commercial in the Western world, so animals were bred and slaughtered purely for their skins. Scruples often went out of the window. The stunning creatures God created for His enjoyment and which reflect His glory became valued only for the skins on their backs. This was fashion vanity at its most obscene. We have all been sickened by reports of indiscriminate and merciless killing of animals for fur.

Recently the fur market has begun to collapse. Harrod's fur department has closed down as even among the very rich fur is no longer fashionable. Over the years, pressure groups like Greenpeace, Friends of the Earth and Lynx have campaigned against the fur trade. Gradually people have taken heed and changed.

Way back in 1982, I was arrested with twenty-two other people for demonstrating in the fur department of Manchester's Kendals store. Our protest was a sit-in and we repetitively and imaginatively chanted 'Fur trade out!' The police arrived and told us to get up and go or they'd arrest us, and so everyone got up to go and we were arrested anyway. That evening, just released from police custody, I went to see some friends to tell them what had happened. Over the radio came the verse 'Blessed are those who are persecuted because of righteousness for theirs is the kingdom of heaven.'[5] 'That's for you,' they joked. Later in my bedroom I checked my Bible. I had no idea the verse was one of the Beatitudes. I opened the book randomly and there it was. Now, whether you believe that that was God trying to tell me something or not, I believe that the swing away from wearing fur for *fashion* reasons is something that has the hallmark of God stamped upon it.

Silk is a natural fabric that should have people considering whether they really need wear it. For silkworms are boiled alive in their silk thread cocoons in vats of steaming water so that the unravelling thread can be collected for our use. If people have no qualms about eating lobster which are killed in exactly the same way, then it's not a problem. Otherwise, try to avoid both . . .

Seeing through synthetics

Some people argue that it's better to wear fur and silk than man-made copies. They have a point. Nylons, polyester, rayon and viscose are produced in the laboratory and created from oil. A lot of energy is used in the excavation and production and a lot of pollution is produced.

There are some good points. Polyester cotton and other synthetic/natural mixes are cool, comfortable and light to wear. The drip-dry shirt, despite its whole image shrieking 'synthetic', saves energy on drying and ironing. And the more modern materials which have come out of laboratories are tremendously lightweight, pack up very small, and are ideal for trekking and climbing.

Tights are probably the most environmentally damaging items of clothing worn today. They ladder easily –

sometimes the first time they're worn. They are not easily disposable (in the true sense of the word). And they use up the world's valuable stocks of petroleum.

Fashion designer Anthony Price once remarked that tights were the most space-age of clothing: 'They come out of this little packet and one size fits anybody.' But unfortunately many people have a very space-age mentality towards them. They throw them away as soon as they've got the smallest of holes in them.

But there are ways that girls and women can reduce the destruction without having to resort to dusting their legs with coffee or cocoa powder and tracing a line of kohl from the heel upwards as women did during wartime!

In the winter, wear holed ones under trousers to keep your legs warm, or otherwise use thick cotton or wool ones. If you have a pair in which one leg is laddered and the other undamaged, and another pair exactly the same, cut off the bad legs at the hip. Thread the remaining 'good' leg from one pair through the hole left by the 'amputated' leg of the other and you have a new pair of tights! If a pair really is beyond repair, cut it into pieces small enough for stuffing soft toys, pin cushions, etc. Where you have sections of a leg that aren't laddered, cut them out from the leg and use for wrist or ankle warmers. Or sew one open end of a section to the other one so you have a circular tube. Use it as a hair band or to hold a ponytail. Dye the pieces in your favourite colours to brighten them up. And in the summer, bare all. Let your legs tan and go without a cover-up.

Stockings are a good alternative. Buy up pairs of your favourite colour in sales, so that if one breaks, you simply put the other back into the pool! Or use socks! There is now an unlimited variety of patterns and designs available, and picked to match an outfit they can look very smart. When clothes are as environmentally expensive as tights, then we need to be wise and all the more resourceful in how we use God's resources.

Natural product
Natural fabrics such as cotton, linens and wool adapt better to a climate and they feel better close to your skin. They allow your body to breathe and communicate in a very simple way how God has directly provided us with the protection we need.

And they are self-renewing and hard-wearing, and come in such a variety of weights that they will see us throughout the year. They may cost more than synthetics, but they'll still be looking good years ahead from now.

The raw materials are designed for us to wear them without having necessarily to resort to large-scale industrial processes – though today many do. Cotton has become a cash crop, and sheep can be injured in the shearing, and wools are becoming synthetic or mixed fibred like more modern materials.

Increasingly unbleached cotton is becoming fashionable. Up to now, we've liked our 'whites right', but getting something pure white means it's got to be bleached, which adds pollutants to the environment. Off-white is becoming okay. Which is good on the washing front too. As long as your clothes are clean, it shouldn't matter too much if the colours have run a bit or if the tones have lost their sharpness. Just make sure the washing powder you use is Ecover or Ark with no harmful chemicals to add to our water system.

Style recycle
What if you've grown out of your clothes, or when it comes to practical skills you're all fingers and thumbs? You can have an equally interesting time checking out the charity stores. They're useful too for places to deposit your old clothes, though some are choosy about the things they'll take. Jumble sales are also great places for giving

and taking. Set yourself a spending limit: 'I'm not going to spend more than £1.50 here.' It adds to the fun!

It's amazing the bargains you'll discover, and you'll come to wonder why you ever bothered paying over the odds for mass-produced style from your local fashion store. It's great fun rummaging in charity shops and nearly-news and at markets and jumble sales for low-price designs that can be worn as they are or hitched up or in to create original outfits. Of course it helps if you've got dressmaking skills, but on your travels you're just as likely to find good quality ready-to-wear.

Some charity shops have levels of quality. Items handed over at a shop in one town could end up earning more being sold in a shop in a wealthier district, though this isn't always the case. My best-ever bargain has to be a tremendously smart hardly-worn Hardy Amies Prince of Wales check jacket that cost me £3.50 in a suburban Barnardos. It's seen many a job interview and it really raises eyebrows when hanging on office coatstands. Otherwise, Oxfam's branch in London's St John's Wood is the *crème-de-la-crème* of its stores. Though you'll pay more for the clothes there, you'll be buying designer labels at knock-down prices, and helping people of the Third World into the bargain.

Being able to pick and choose clothes so cheaply and easily helps us to develop our own personal taste of colour and shape, and our imagination. Of course we'll occasionally make the odd gruesome mistake and come away with an outfit which just isn't us — but we can take it back to be bought by somebody else (which earns the 'good cause' twice the money for the one garment!), and it won't be an overly expensive mistake.

Make a vow to have a wardrobe turn-out twice a year — spring and autumn. It helps to develop your dress sense, stimulates your imagination for the coming season and enables you to spot your mistakes and learn from them. And once you get into the habit of giving away clothes still in good condition to those who'll make good use of them, you become more aware of your own wants and needs when it comes to dressing up.

Of course we all need to wear clothes, but from a Christian perspective, you begin to wonder if you need so many. Said John the Baptist, 'A man with two tunics should share with him who has none, and the one who has food should do the same.'[6]

God doesn't necessarily want us dressed in sackcloth and ashes, but He wants us to be resourceful in the way we dress. Once you have the basic wardrobe, then you can begin to take John's words seriously. After all, do you really need two winter coats?

Hand-me-downs

Keep an eye on what your family is discarding. Your grandfather may not be able to imagine why you want his old cardigan, but it might be just the thing you're looking for. And, moreover, you'll save £20 or £30 you might have spent trying to achieve the same effect. Some clothes look better the older they get, too. An original flying jacket is a real find, a 'little black dress' from the Thirties or Forties, handknitted jumpers from the same or a later period. . . Does anything remain of your parents' Fifties and Sixties wardrobes? My sister, a family friend and I, having sat and listened to our mothers tell us about the Fifties dresses they wore at the time, all bemoaned the fact that they hadn't thought it necessary to keep them for any daughters they might have!

The shock of the new

Of course, there are times when need to buy new. But funnily enough, the more open you are to thinking about the clothes you wear and being more resourceful, the more difficult it is to buy new clothes! Instead they become accessories, completing an outfit. It's more fun totting up the cost of your clothes and finding how little it comes to — and surprising people by revealing that the outfit they admire is all your own work or, as I tag some of my second–hand stuff, 'an Oxfam special'.

I just don't buy basics brand new. Shirts, trousers and skirts can all be picked up in good nick second-hand. Even for special occasions it can be difficult buying new. Of the four weddings I went to in 1989, I wore second-hand outfits to three of them and a dress I'd had gathering dust in the back of my wardrobe for at least four years to the fourth. (None of the weddings, I hasten to add, were mine!) I've been to a Cambridge Ball in a matching cocktail dress and jacket which together cost 10p from a jumble sale, and nobody batted an eyelid.

But I *do* have new clothes. And I find that God has modified my tastes so that I tend to keep my clothes until they fall apart. I buy clothes that I like, rather than ones that are 'in' this season. And they have to practically jump off the rack and scream at me for me to buy them. They have to prove themselves.

T-shirts are probably the most versatile of clothes. These days they're so cheap (a discount store close to home sells them for £1.99 each, two for £3), and available in so many different colours that you can stockpile and have real fun. Choose ones to brighten up your wardrobe. Wear layers of ones of different colours and tones, and roll up sleeves, pull up necks and pull down hems so that a clashing or vibrant mix of shades shows through. Buy large and extra large to use as night shirts, head wraps, as over-shirts or dresses over swimsuits on blistering hot days and to cover up on cool summer nights. . . And roll up plenty and cram them into a suitcase so you don't have to worry what to wear on your hols.

T-shirts also bring social and political issues into the fashion arena. Many charities — Oxfam, Traidcraft, Tear Fund, Lynx and Greenpeace — now have their own, and by wearing one not only do you stretch your views across your chest, but help the cause too.

But don't feel you've got to wear the T-shirt to help a charity. Don't be buttonholed into buying something you don't want and will never wear. You shouldn't have to buy something to help somebody else – whether it's T-shirts, records, red noses, concert tickets or a little paper sticker to put on your lapel. Not only do these use up valuable resources, but you're also shouting about how good you are to help somebody else.

And that's not the way Jesus wanted us to do things: 'Be careful not to do your acts of righteousness before men, to be seen by them. If you do, you will have no reward from your Father in heaven.

'So when you give to the needy, do not announce it with trumpets, as the hypocrites do in the synagogues and on the streets, to be honoured by men. I tell you the truth, they have received their reward in full. But when you give to the needy, do not let your left hand know what your right hand is doing, so that your giving may be in secret. Then your Father, who sees what is done in secret, will reward you.'[7]

Just hand over your money and let them keep the change.

Try to avoid buying clothes at full price. Sales are so frequent these days that you shouldn't have to. Be patient and learn to spot clothes that won't sell at the price that's being asked. I once tried on a suit which I knew suited me. It cost £40 but it was made of lightweight material and was unlined – so I guessed that the price would drop. I waited a few weeks and snapped it up for half price. Put the money you save aside for a worthy cause.

Think classic – jeans, white shirts, plain T-shirts, crew neck jerseys, trenchcoats, plain neat skirts. . . Go for neutral colours that can be jazzed up – beige or black with red, stone or grey with gold. . . Take a classic and add a twist of a wild accessory. Buy an unusual or ultra stylish pair of shoes that stand out. Make these the focal point of a dark or plain outfit. And remember that style works best when it's understated.

It's a step of faith to put your clothing into God's hands and aim to live with less. The next time you buy yourself an item of clothing, you could give away a similar item of clothing you already have at home so that you're replacing, not increasing your wardrobe.

It's a step of faith too to ask God to provide for your clothing needs from jumble sales and charity shops. Try it on your friends as well. Give them clothes you've made, or those which are in good condition but don't suit you. Develop a clothes-swap system that saves money and resources, and develops friendships.

Don't be a slave to fashion. Use it to serve God instead.

ACTION STATION

List:

Things I look good in	*Things I should avoid*
1	1 ....
2	2 ....
3	3 ....
4	4 ....
5	5 ....

Colours that suit me: ....

Outfits to make or alter

1 ....
2 ....
3 ....
4 ....
5 ....

Money spent on clothes	*Money saving ideas*
....	....
....	....
....	....

7

Consuming Passions

We live in a consumer culture. All round we are besieged by adverts in magazines and on TV screens telling us that by buying a certain product we'll be better people, full of life and attractive to others.

As Christians we know that this is plainly not true. Coke is not 'it', nor the Real Thing, come to that. Material possessions do not make you a wiser, happier or more beautiful person in the true sense.

The rich and famous people splashed across the papers apparently have everything, but many of them have nothing. Their worth is measured by the cars they drive, the designer clothes they wear, the mansions they live in, but few know where they're going. 'What good,' asked Jesus, 'will it be for a man if he gains the whole world, yet forfeits his soul?'[1]

And knowing this truth helps us see that we don't need half of what's on offer in high street and department stores. Sure, a lot of it's tempting, and it can be fun to go window shopping pointing out what we'd splash out on if we had the money. But by looking to God to check our real needs, it's easier to walk on by.

Teenagers in particular are under a great deal of pressure to spend on clothes, music and cosmetics to 'keep up' with other teenagers. Since the 1950s, when they stopped dressing like their parents, young people have been targeted as consumers in their own right and sold looks, sounds and heroes. Even the high street banks have now got in on the act and attract younger and younger investors with gimmicky magazines and other giveaways.

You've got to be strong to resist the pull of consumerism. But if you start to think about whether you really do need a new outfit/album/computer program and reduce your spending on these goods, you'll find a new freedom. You can wait awhile before you have to get an after-school job to keep you in the money. Though Saturday jobs are useful experience both jobwise and socially, the flipside of the coin is that they're tiring, take up one of your break days and prevent you from taking time out to spend it in more artistic, creative and relaxing pursuits.

Buying power

But what if you want to get a new record or buy a book — or a new 'wardrobe'? Stop awhile to look at how this can be a more Green experience. The peculiar thing about records and books is that we know *exactly* what we're looking for. But even so, we can find that our enjoyment of each is expanded when we take advantage of some of the alternative ways to get hold of them.

Second-hand record shops, bargain bins and charity stores are great for rummaging for records. The fun point about all these is that the records are very cheap, so that if any of them do turn out to be duff, it doesn't matter too much. It means you can experiment by listening to different sounds — a bit of classical, some jazz, stuff from the Sixties or whenever and whoever — and broaden your tastes and your outlook.

When you're in your teens it's easy to get very particular about the music you listen to. Chances are, you only like one kind and nothing else matches it. When my mates Naomi, Frances, Claire and Sally were into the mod scene and ska, I was into Gary Numan, Orchestral Manoeuvres In The Dark, and on Sunday nights me and my sis went posing at 'Ziggys' (cough) at the St Moritz Club in Wardour Street. And apart from my Cliff discs I hardly bought any other type of music than electronic stuff. Now, I regret not seeing The Specials with my mates (whether they regret not seeing Gazza Numan or Ultravox is another matter!). And I recently picked up a cheap copy of the The Beat's first album and thoroughly enjoy it.

And another thing that's rather nice about secondhand records is that they've been through other fans' hands. I have records from the Fifties and early Sixties, and I know that the people who bought them in the first place, whoever they are, got enjoyment out of them as I do when I listen today. The odd click (and there are very few, if any) and the slightly worn sleeve are part of the record's history.

And when your tastes *do* change, but maybe there's one track on an album which you still like, tape that track and give the record away. It's a good idea once in a while to go through your collection and weed out the no-hopers so you can take them to a charity shop or give them to friends.

Books are similar. It's so easy to accumulate them. Work your way through the ones you have, and if they don't do anything to you then pass them on. But be careful with old children's books that still mean something to you, but which you understandably feel you're too old for. You can end up throwing them out and then regretting it for years afterwards. If children's books are written well they can appeal to all ages.

And when it comes to books, this is where libraries come in. The nice thing about public libraries is that you have access to a startling range of fiction and non-fiction literature, particularly if you're in the larger cities.

Libraries are very important in a culture that is based on text, because they enable people who otherwise couldn't afford many books to be able to read plenty. And they're a very clever way of reusing books and spreading the joy of reading. I know some libraries, particularly those under left-wing authorities, which choose not to stock Christian books because it's argued that they're biased. They'll happily stock books that mirror their own world view. It's up to us to visit our local library and request Christian books to get them onto the shelves and available to a wider audience.

Libraries allow you to 'try out' different writers, to pick 'n' choose without spending anything. And if you find that you really do enjoy a particular author or book, then you can save up and buy the books. If you're philosophical enough, you don't even need to do that. Certainly, having a book is convenient — it's there when you want it. But if you can't afford one, at least with a library service you know that that's not the end of the story.

Whatever you're buying, it's your attitude towards it that's important. Think of alternative sources. Wander round markets, antique shops and second-hand stores. What you'll pick up will be individual, reasonably priced compared to the shop bought article, and fun to find. But remember, too, that you can get carried away with the buying business, and that materialism can be as much about stocking up on lots of cheap, used products as about only ever buying new.

You come to learn about quality. You reach the point where you're just not prepared to pay for shoddy workmanship and cheap finishings in new products. If you can get it cheaper secondhand and it does the job just as well, then why buy new? And as my friend Juliet and I agree, you can get so used to buying stuff really cheaply, that you simply object to paying £20 for a shirt or over a fiver for a haircut.

I don't know if it's just the way I am, but one reason why I hold back on the brand new is that if I didn't, I wouldn't be satisfied with a lot of what you can buy in the High Street. I have an extravagant streak in me, and so maybe I keep an extra strong hold on the reins. But then, because I go for quality, I should hope that my stuff lasts for years. I was browsing once in the Bentalls store in Ealing when I overheard one elderly lady say to her friend, 'The thing about getting old is that all your belongings start to fall apart, and you have to replace them.' I'd be happy if my possessions lasted as long as that!

Packing case

It's not just what we buy, it's what we buy it in. It's difficult to buy anything without a wrapper around it, except perhaps fruit and veg. Many greengrocers still use the traditional method of tumbling spuds into your basket, wrapping them up in newspaper, or putting fruit in plain brown paper bags which have as many further uses as you're willing to come up with.

You have to be confident when it comes to refusing packaging, but it gets easier. Do stick to your guns. Even in The Body Shop I had to stress to one shop assistant that though its bags are made from recycled paper, I still didn't want one. Technically, a receipt should be your only necessary proof of purchase.

Take a plastic bag with you when you go shopping so that you don't need another. Look out for products in glass containers — roll-on deodorant bottles can be washed out, filled with paint or ink and used as massive ballpoint pens! The Body Shop has a useful refill service for its bottled products. Look for items sold in cardboard boxes instead of plastic film or moulding.

We hear all this fuss about aerosols and the ozone hole, and manufacturers assuring us that *theirs* is ozone-friendly. You can live perfectly happily without using an aerosol at all. From an early age I knew that aerosols were difficult to get rid of and that you weren't meant to burn them or puncture them. And I am certain that the ozone hole was known about in the early seventies, for I'm sure that was the other reason why they weren't considered a good idea. Anyway, don't throw your aerosols away; just don't buy them.

Green consuming

What is notable about the environmental movement this time around is that it's all about buying. I don't altogether understand why a chain store like the Body Shop is hailed as wonderfully Green. The cosmetic industry is a tremendously luxurious one – you just don't need a lot of what's on offer. Personally I feel that shops like The Hire Shop and heel bars are much more Green in concept.

The Sixties and early Seventies concentrated a more on a sort of 'made-do-and-mend' mentality and a back-to-basics lifestyle. The bestselling *Green Consumer Guide* lists a certain brand of champagne among the acceptable products . . .

There is no sacrifice this time around. The word is regarded as rather negative in Green circles; you're meant to emphasise the positives. With Christianity, of course it's worth emphasising the positives, but sacrifice is a basic part. After all, where would we be without Jesus' ultimate sacrifice? And though good comes later and hope is stirred anew, we have to be prepared to tighten our belts at least just a little so that we become more complete people.

The Green followers this time around have been encouraged to carry on consuming, as long as it's Green consuming. Certainly you can make positive buys of products which are not tested on animals and which are 'environmentally sound' or 'ozone friendly' but you can make just as many positive decisions by not buying the product in the first place.

ACTION STATION
- Read:
  Born to Shop By Mike Starkey (Monarch, 1989).
  The Young Consumer Guide by John Elkington and Julia Hailes (Gollancz, 1990).

The Green Consumer Guide by John Elkington and Julia Hailes (Gollancz, 1989).

Consumer's Guide to the Protection of the Environment by Jonathon Holliman (Pan/Ballantine, 1971).

- If something you buy has excessive packaging, send the packaging back to the manufacturers with a polite note explaining why you're not happy with their produce. And congratulate those companies which use Greener packaging.

- Subscribe to *New Consumer*[2] and *Ethical Consumer*[3] magazines.

- When you go out, take less money with you so that you're not tempted to buy things you don't need or want.

- Make a list of the last consumer goods you bought:

  1 ....
  2 ....
  3 ....
  4 ....
  5 ....

  What made you buy them? Go through each product and recall whether it was: Need/Seen on advert/Friends had one/Trendy/Everyone's got one/Very few people have got them . . .

- Is there something you need? Pray that God will provide it through a second-hand or charity shop so that you can put less pressure on His earth.

8

Garden Party

What ever kind of home you live in, try and cultivate a piece of land, whether it's a plant pot, a window box or acres of ground. Caring for the soil and what grows out of it, waiting and watching life uncurl, helps us value life more.

Growing things helps us see the world from God's point of view and understand the truth of Jesus' words: 'I am the true vine, and my Father is the gardener. He cuts off every branch that bears no fruit, while every branch that does bear fruit He prunes so that it will be even more fruitful.'[1]

It works both ways. Such words not only show that our faith needs to be cultivated and to 'bear fruit', but that it's good and right to prune, to coppice and to cut back living things.

Spending a week one summer coppicing with the British Trust for Conservation Volunteers, I found myself questioning whether it was right to chop down plants like gorse bushes and birch trees so that other trees could flourish. Now I'm certain it is. It's all right too to pull ivy from a tree trunk it's strangling so that the tree can survive.

'The Lord God took the man and put him in the Garden of Eden to work it and take care of it.'[2] Our place in looking after God's world is to train it so that the best comes from it. Our job is not always to 'let nature take its course' (though sometimes it's right just to let things be), whether that's in connection with plants or animals. As Christ's ambassadors we must be ready to intervene in a loving way, as He did, if something or

74

somebody needs our help.

If you've ever watched the Follyfoot TV series, you'll know that there's a charred 'lightning' tree in the stable grounds. It became a tradition among those who worked on the programme to throw a bucket of water over the blackened wood whenever they passed it. After ages of doing this, the tree sent out new green shoots – and the cast were suitably amazed. Whoever started the tradition must have had a tiny seed of hope that the tree would regrow. That seed grew in others' hearts as well. For if there had been no hope, the act of throwing a bucket of water would have not only have been, but *felt*, a waste of time. Hope spread and was excitingly fulfilled. Maybe the tree would have lived without the extra water it was given. But maybe it wouldn't.

Patch of Ground
If you have access to a garden, find a small corner to cultivate. Don't bother at this stage with packets of seeds. From my own experience the chances of growing anything closely resembling the bright floral collection on the front of the packet is quite remote. Instead use cuttings from other plants or seeds that are already sending out shoots. I have to admit to not being particularly green-fingered; I haven't got the patience. But tough plants that don't

need much looking after and just get on and grow suit
me fine. Bulbs that sprout up year after year – tulips,
daffs and crocuses — look great among grass. Make a
vow never to buy plants from a garden centre (where
they're often hideously expensive). Instead, when friends
come to visit, ask them to bring a cutting or a root of
something from their garden. You'll soon have a garden
stocked with memories as well as flowers and shrubs.

Fruit and vegetable plants are great to grow because
there's an end result to encourage you to look after them
for next year. There's something very enjoyable – and
cheap! – about eating food you've grown yourself. A
potato left over from a potato-printing art class which
I brought home from school and buried in the garden
produced a lovely batch of fresh new spuds. As a child,
my brother Mick planted a peach stone which grew into
a tree and occasionally bore a peach or two. I can't
remember eating the fruit, but I remember being struck
at how something like that could grow from a small boy
putting a seed in the English soil.

And on you patch of land, don't feel it's got to look
like something out of *Country Life* magazine. Weeds are
plants that are growing in the wrong place. Nettles might
look a mess to some people; they hint of neglected land.
But they are here for a purpose. Sure, they sting, like the
rose has its thorns – the pain of the fallen world – but
nettles can be picked to make soup, and they attract red
admiral butterflies to your garden. They are also one of
the richest sources of nutrient for the soil – a heap of
cut-down nettles added to your compost is an organic
gardener's favourite. Beauty and joyful life grow from
the tough and common 'weed'.

Alloted space

If your garden is too small but you'd like to grow food,
then contact your local council to see whether they've a
small allotment you can hire. Tending your crops you'll

meet other people of all ages and swap food and advice, and you'll learn to understand the art of gardening. You'll be able to experiment growing different fruit and vegetables and cultivate them organically, without using chemical fertilisers.

Pond life

A pond attracts wildlife to a garden whether in the city or the countryside. If you don't have a garden, see if your school will allow you and your friends to build one as part of a nature study or biology lesson. With a couple of people to help, a pond is not difficult to dig. Richard Spurgeon's excellent *Ecology* explains how with easy-to-follow instructions and helpful illustrations.[3] A pond dug in a horseshoe shape lengthens the amount of bank available for plants and for shoreline creatures to lay their eggs.

And wildlife certainly does come. Frogs and toads looking for a damp place to stay in town will home in on your waterhole. Insects and waterbugs – boatmen, dragonfly and aquatic plants — should thrive. And you'll be helping protect the UK's vulnerable pond life. Take part in the Pondwatch survey to help Watch and the Wildfowl and Wetland Trust gauge the state of the nation's pond life.[4] Ponds are an important part of the environment that need our protection.

Says Richard Spurgeon: 'Ponds are much less common today than they were forty years ago. Many have been filled in or have grown over. This is most unfortunate for their inhabitants. Some plants and animals only live in certain habitats. When those disappear, so do they.'[5]

Ponds are a very localised part of the environment, and to some people their fate will seem unimportant when compared with, say, the destruction of the tropical rainforests. But like all of God's creation, lose Britain's ponds and the world suffers for that loss.

Creative use of green space

Don't be put off if you haven't a garden to experiment
with. Look out for green spaces close to where you live
– not only parks and grass verges, but scrubland and
derelict areas, too. Wildlife grows rapidly in neglected
places and it's free for you to appreciate.

Like Adam and Eve tending the Garden of Eden, make
it your job to look after this space, whether that's just
clearing away the rubbish or cutting away the dead wood.
Get a group of Christian friends together to pray for it
– and pray there too.

Prayer can be thrilling out of doors. You're there in
the natural world which God created, opening your heart
to Him. In Austria, along the alpine roadsides are dotted
little Catholic shrines of the crucified Christ that act as
a reminder of whose world it is. Standing in the heart
of the fresh and largely unspoilt Austrian countryside,
they don't seem out of place at all.

I once spent a week on a Scripture Union young
people's 'Intake Week' at a site among the conifers of
the Quantocks. Each day during the seven days of
sunshine we would worship at a little outdoor chapel as
birds sang around us, the wind breezed between the trees
and a brook trickled over rocks past our tree trunk
'pews'. At the end of the week, each of us was asked to
pack a mental 'suitcase' of experiences from the week to
take away with us. The chapel in the open air was one
of my favourite loads.

It might seem a bit strange to pray for a patch of land,
riverbank or garden you're looking after, but these places
need God's protection. It's not enough to work on it and
appreciate the beauty of the Creation. Part of 'tending
the Garden' is about praying for it, too.

This was brought home to me when I was put up by
workmates in Hounslow, West London, while searching
for accommodation. Hounslow is an interesting town in
that though only a few miles from Heathrow Airport,

run through with traffic and acting as a regular suburban edge of London, it's full of untouched green spaces. Walk along a street, turn a corner, and there will be a patch of land run wild.

One residential street on my way to the town centre contained a small meadow. A house had been knocked down and in its place was thriving a striking array of grasses, my favourite 'weed' rosebay willowherb, nettles and shrubs. Butterflies fluttered around this oasis and birds nested in this sanctuary. It was a beautiful site.

One sunny day I decided to take a picture of this patch of land. But when I got there, a mechanical digger was biting at the soil. The colour of the street was turned to mud. I almost wept. But I tried to be philosophical; it was a residential street and people needed housing — and rather there than on the edge of London. But what was built in place of the meadow wasn't a house. It was the Hounslow Spiritualist Centre. And now whenever I pass that building advertising its clairvoyant meetings and psychic groups I am saddened at how a small part of God's creation became overgrown with evil.

A tale of a garden

The story of Man starts in a Garden where humanity is given the job of looking after it for its Creator. But humanity wants power and so is banished from Eden. And the task of caring for the soil and what grows out of it becomes backbreaking work.

> Cursed is the ground because of you; through painful toil you will eat of it all the days of your life.
> It will produce thorns and thistles for you, and you will eat the plants of the field.
> By the sweat of your brow you will eat your food until you return to the ground, since from it you were taken; for dust you are and to dust you will return.[6]

But what happens in a garden later brings new hope. The garden where Jesus was resurrected and escaped from the tomb is the garden where our thoughts should be focused. The image we carry in our heads from pictures in childhood Bibles and Easter celebrations is a garden of light and sunshine, of spring blooms and rockeries and a stone path leading to the open tomb. And it is where Mary Magdalene, the first person to see Jesus alive after His burial, mistook Him for a gardener. She wasn't far wrong. For Jesus is the one true Gardener, watching over us, training us so that we grow in the right direction, cutting back the dead wood.

It's something to bear in mind when we're busy in our gardens. As we dig at the soil, grit our teeth and turn over chunks of mud, get our hands dirty and gently put in plants, we're growing, too. We're learning how to care for a tiny corner of God's vast creation and to help nurture new life. And the effort and energy we put in strengthens us physically, mentally and spiritually.

Whatever the size of your patch of land, the texture of the soil beneath your fingers and the minute shoots springing up — if only some cress seeds on an old flannel! — help us understand a small something of what it means to be like God, created in His image. That we can never fully understand, but the image in our heads of God as Gardener tending us as we amateur gardeners tend the soil is surely God-given and one to dwell on as we potter among the plants.

ACTION STATION

- Collect seeds of all types and plant them on waste ground and areas that could do with a bit of colour and variety.

- Use household waste of fruit and veg peelings and newspaper to start building a compost heap. Check at your local library for a book on how to build one.

- Plant a seed in a pot and watch it grow. Carefully tend it and when it gets big enough, transplant it into the ground and keep on caring for it. Use a seed of a sunflower, walnut or horse chestnut − or an acorn − so that you'll really notice the transformation.

9

School of Thought

As you spend a good deal of your time in education, and the same again in work, and it's the place where you meet your friends and forge your future, it's important that Green thinking and your Christian faith have an influence here.

Like your home, your school, college or workplace is a small world where a group of people have to work as a team and share facilities. Think about the possible ways you can reuse and recycle materials and how from day-to-day students or employees must be encouraged not to be wasteful if money and energy are to be saved. At my school there were 'Save it' stickers stuck next to all the light switches. Probably your school or workplace doesn't still have *those*, but why not check if lights really need to be on and switch off accordingly.

Desk duty

Your school desk could well be, or was, a fine example of the art of reusing resources. Many have seen generations of schoolchildren pour over exam papers, and bear the scrawl and carvings of past frustrations.

Your own desk at school, college or office is the place from where you can start making positive Green choices and actions. Just look inside it. Is there a way of cutting down on the paper you use? Do your text books or exercise books need covers? Don't buy expensive wrapping paper to do the job, but use newspaper, glossy magazine paper or a large paper bag, which will be just as good. Some people when handed a text book which still wears the jacket of the previous owner rip it off and put on their own coverings. Don't do that, but stick on a pic of whatever you like to personalise it instead.

School kids do funny things with exercise books. I don't know how I managed it, but I've still got a number of old, practically unused exercise books from my junior school days! I also recall two girls in my class, Gillian and Rachel, who wrote in pencil in their rough books and then when they got to the end they'd go back and start over again only this time writing in biro. All this was so that at the end of the year, because we got a rough book at the start of each term anyway, they'd each have one they hadn't used. Don't ask me what they did with the spare copy.

You could go to those lengths to be Green, after all the method worked for us. Though we missed the point a bit. The thing is to return the spare copies so that somebody else can use them instead of hoarding them, instead of hoarding them, which doesn't benefit anybody. Every so often when I remember where they are I drag out an old battered one and use it for rough notes.

There's no need ever to use brand new rough paper, if you see what I mean. You should always be able to find some scrap to scribble on. Many offices provide desk diaries for their staff. Don't throw yours out when the year ends. There are bound to be some pages that are not written on. Use yours as a notebook.

The further up the school system you go, the more rules are relaxed. Eventually it'll probably be okay for you to use files, and this is something carried over into student life and work. Because so many offices are replacing their ancient filing systems with computers and word processors, there are a lot of old files being thrown out, especially the wide lever arch ones.

If you or someone you know works in an office, see if you can get hold of some. Otherwise, if ever you're passing a skip outside an office, just peep over the edge and see if there's anything worth salvaging. That's where

I've retrieved most of my files from, and old they are, but they do the job.

File paper is far easier to use Greenly than exercise books and other sizes of paper. You can now get blocks of A4 recycled file paper in W.H.Smiths, but remember to use both sides of the paper. If you ink in the lines on a sheet of lined paper, you'll be able to put that behind a piece of white paper that's only been used on one side, and write straight. Again, ask a friend who works in an office if there's any paper that's blank on one side that they can collect for you, or look out for it yourself. It's great for sketching on and for photocopying and rough print-outs too.

I use A4 paper that's been used on *both* sides as backing paper for cuttings and pictures cut from magazines. If you're doing a course such as Art and Design where you're encouraged to collect pictures that interest you and go to exhibitions, such paper is very useful – and doesn't cost anything.

Some time in your school life you'll probably want to write with a fountain pen. A lot of people gravitate to ink pens when they start secondary school, and then end up with biros as the're far less of a hassle. But there's a lot going for the fountain pen. If you get a good one with a rubber inside, instead of a cartridge pen, it'll last far longer than any cheap biro. It also makes your writing look much better and at work, or for college, is a smart alternative to the ballpoint pen.

Pentel pens might produce nice strong and dark lettering, but in my experience they're the most inefficient pens around. I lost count of the number of times I'd be at full flow and then I'd press the pen against the paper just a little too hard and the ball point would disappear inside the pen, never to come out. There was no option but to throw the thing away.

To carry all your gear around get a sturdy holdall, or search around markets for chic satchels and miniature cases. Be sure to scour the cheapo stores, too. Whenever I use my French 'briefcase', people comment on how stylish it is. I bought it eight years ago for about £3.50 from Uniprix, the French equivalent of Woolies, during their annual sale of 'back to school' goods. It could do with a few stitches, but apart from that it's served me well. Just don't end up resorting to placcy bags that don't last any time at all and need to be replaced far too often.

Room change

Though schools are run fairly formally and you can feel pretty powerless at times, there is always an informal network among classmates. The same largely goes for college and work. As a Christian interested in Green living it's here in particular that you can make an impact.

Passing exciting books around the class so that everybody gets a share of the action is common in schools. Often it'll be some saucy dog-eared tome that's considered very daring to read, but it doesn't have to be. In my class, Elizabeth, our token very committed Christian, circulated copies of *The Cross and the Switchblade* and *Run Baby Run* round 4B and everyone was riveted. As more and more people are going Green, why not try and get your friends to read some of the books that appear in the list at the end of this book?

This 'library system' is a great way of sharing if you don't mind too much about the condition your books will be returned in. If you're going to lend any of your possessions, be warned that rarely will you get them back looking the same as when they were lent. It is the same when you take the time to listen to friends, or help a person in need. It changes you. It's what being friendly is all about, and is part of the sacrifice of Christian giving.

Let friends know that you are concerned about Green issues and that you're open to receiving recyclable goods to take down to the bottle/paper/can bank. See if you can get a group of them involved too. After a while people will start coming to you with their rubbish, knowing that you want to do something with it.

Why not wander around your school grounds, local park or college grounds during your lunch hour and keep your eyes open for nature. And aim to get your friends interested too. Artist Mark Boyle and his family have spent years taking a close look at their environment and noting the changes through texts, moulds, sculptures, photographs and paintings. Green sculptor Andy Goldsworthy creates striking images in the environment using nothing but natural materials. Leaves are pinned into intricate shapes with thorns. Richard Long traces pathways from rocks and wood. Check your library for books on their work and experiment on a patch of ground close to where you work or study.

Look closely at stones, plants, trees, fungi, the local architecture. Identify the different species. Check up on local history and how your town has grown and changed. At school we were always taught that the glaciers of the Ice Age stopped just up the road from the school at Northwood's Haste Hill. I'm afraid I always found that a bit unbelievable, a bit too coincidental . . . And our town featured in the Doomsday Book too. Get to know the place where you live or work.

Lesson to learn

If you're still at school, have a word with your form teacher and ask if the class could organise a Green session, by looking at the materials everybody throws away and finding alternative uses, and through discussion of the issues.

Maybe your art teacher would be interested in encouraging recycled art. During my sixth form somehow one entire A-level art class got hooked on collage – we couldn't look at a still life or create an image without thinking of producing the textures in 3D. Papier-mâché is a good way of using up newspaper and a cheap material for sculptures of any size. One of my early teachers, a Mr Milsome, had a thing about making models out of silver foil. In fact, any material that's fairly malleable can be moulded into new forms.

Whether you're at school or college, check out lessons and lectures where you can use your Christian Green worldview. Geography introduces you to an area's physical and social landscape which is valuable in literally understanding the shapes and patterns of God's world around you. I can still remember the thrill of identifying my first 'live' interlocking spurs. Suddenly, out in the countryside what I'd learnt in the classroom clicked into place.

Biology lessons can be fascinating too. I'm afraid I got lost around spirogyra, but I can still draw a marvellous alveolus! And the other sciences – physics and chemistry – open up the physical world to reveal how its pieces fit together and react with each other.

Volunteer to help the lab assistant set up experiments. If there are laboratory 'pets' – locusts, worms, mice – ask if you can look after them. Of course some people are very anti animals being caged at all, which is fair enough. But if your school does have them, it's important that a caring person has responsibility for them.

Or if you find the whole idea really offputting, why not get a petition together to request that no animals be used in school experiments, and that live creatures are therefore taken out of the classroom. These days you should be able to refuse to take part in dissections. The GCSEs make what you have to study far more flexible and you can avoid fiddling around with a dead animal. It's really not necessary to slice through a cow's eye to cut out the lens, or to play around with a sheep's organs. There are so many well-produced videos around that there's no need for school students to do any cut-ups.

And if there are unGreen practices at college or work

that you're not happy with, why not bring up the issue at a union meeting? Some Christians are terrified of getting involved in anything as worldly as politics. When I was employed as editor of Manchester Poly's paper *PULP*, one Christian actually asked how I could be working for a student union which promoted gay rights. Another told me they weren't going to vote for Labour in the local elections for the same single reason. Christians need to roll up their sleeves and get into the political arena. Your place of work or study is an ideal place to start.

You should get a good grounding of faith from which to start moving in R.E. classes. If your teachers are Christians they're hopefully already tuned into using stimulating materials that deal with today's important issues. Tear Fund has a useful Resource Catalogue from which they can order posters, videos and information packs focusing on the Third World, including one aimed specifically at GCSE students. An R.E. teacher who prefers to cover a wide range of 'comparative religions' might be interested in getting in touch with the World Wide Fund for Nature (WWF).

Over the past few years, the WWF has become increasingly involved in promoting a Green consciousness among followers of the five world religions of Christianity, Judaism, Buddhism, Islam and Hinduism, and it reports on what representatives of the different faiths are doing. Although the WWFs promotion of multi-faith creation worship sessions is not acceptable to evangelical Christians, there is much practical knowledge to be learnt from people of different religions. And for a class or workplace discussion about a spiritual approach to the environment, the WWF material is a helpful starting point.

But if you find that the spiritual emphasis gets too caught up in the 'all roads lead to God, let's all join together in prayer, if it works for you that's fine by me' syndrome, then take a breather and bring the Green issue up at your next Christian Union meeting.

Other Christians might not be as interested in the environment as you, but it's got to the point now that like it or not, Christians must think about it. You've probably noticed that a lot of people you mix with who do care about the planet are looking for their answers in the very attractive but very misleading New Age movement. Christians have got to be able to show them Jesus cares as much about the world as they do. Advertise your CU meeting. Ask along the Greens you know to hear what Christians have got to say.

And pray that a Green *and* Christian voice will be heard in your school, college or workplace, and that friends will be drawn to the hope for the earth that knowing Jesus brings.

ACTION STATION

- Make a list of all the Green changes – small and large – you'd like to see in your work/study environment, and set about achieving them.

- Make sure your Green activities at home and study/work interact. If you've A4 envelopes at home that you'll never use, take them to work where they might be more useful. You can have too many empty yogurt cartons. Take them to school for use as paint and water pots in art lessons.

- There's a lot of emphasis on schools going Green. Make sure you're part of the action. If you're at college or work, aim to spread Green ideas beyond your immediate group.

10

Full Employment

However much you put it off, there comes a time when you have to think seriously about what you're going to do with your life. For Christians, that doesn't necessarily mean settling for a career we'll stick to until we're pensioned off. Certainly some people are suited to the 'one life, one firm' set-up, but that's not right for all of us. God has a plan for each one of our individual personalities which in fact widens our options for what to do.

When a Careers Officer suggests to a Christian girl to think about being a secretary as if that's the only path open to her, the girl doesn't have to follow this lead. God knows what we're good at, He's shaped our talents and our interests. He'll put us in a place where He and we can use both.

Green Career
If we've an interest in environmental issues we find that we're drawn to jobs that mirror these interests. There are outdoor posts and campaigning jobs that need people with enthusiasm to fill them.

It helps if you've already been involved with a Green group. Join your local Friends of the Earth and get involved with their campaigns, go for weeks and weekends away with the British Trust for Conservation Volunteers, contact your neighbourhood park keeper and volunteer to help out. If you're particularly interested in birds get in touch with the RSPB for information about reserves and where you can lend a hand.

Not only will you have a very rewarding time and make lots of friends while you're giving your services, but you'll be learning skills and information that will be useful in a full-time environmental job.

And don't avoid doing a bit of admin. and budget planning, if it needs to be done. In my time, I've been down to the last five interviewees for a couple of Friends of the Earth recycling information jobs which I would have dearly loved to have got. I remember vividly being able to answer the questions thrown at me by the FoE bod, but when it came to the questions on funding I just couldn't handle the man from the GLC. And I watched the jobs flutter out of the window.

But if you're fortunate enough to be offered the post you want, be warned. Environmental jobs are notoriously low-paid and long-houred. You work because you're thoroughly committed to what you're doing, and because of that you should find your work thoroughly rewarding.

Getting satisfaction

Wherever you work, job satisfaction is vitally important. If you're frustrated in your post and aren't being stretched, then it's probably time to move on. You can't just switch off your unhappy feelings after work. They bleed into your social life and relationships can suffer as your view of the world turns sour. At that point, if not sooner, it's time to look for another job.

Some people get trapped by the 'God wants me here' syndrome. They believe that they're meant to work for a particular organisation, and that God opened all the doors to get them there. Eventually they realise they're no longer satisfied by the way they're treated and they find that their skills go unused. But they stay on and on, consoling themselves by telling themselves that at least they've got a regular income, and that they enjoy the hours when they're not at work.

Too many people, whether Christian or not, are caught in this type of trap. Yet there's no law that says you must stay in your job no matter how unfulfilling it is. Or that you should work your way up to the top of the firm. Or stay there until you're offered a gold watch. But it's amazing how many people do so, despite overwhelming feelings of unhappiness or indifference.

Oh, what are we working for?

This obviously isn't what God wants in our lives. He takes us somewhere to teach us an important truth about ourselves but I don't believe we have to stick it out until Kingdom comes if we begin to feel we don't fit in any more.

I spent months looking for work and sent out over a hundred job applications after I completed my journalism course. I was offered just one job: as a staff writer on a data and telecommunications magazine. I left after three months, knowing that a) it wasn't really my scene, and b) I didn't want to work for an organisation where I was working simply to put money in the boss's pockets.

But from that experience I realised that any job I do has to have something more. It has to have a purpose beyond commercial interest, of helping people or informing people so that they can be more socially active. I've been fortunate that of the five jobs I have had, four have fitted into this category.

The charity/social work (in the general sense) field of employment is a growing one, and once on the circuit there's no need to get off. You'll generally find not only that the work is rewarding, but that many of the people you work alongside will have a caring and concerned approach to life regardless of their politics or beliefs.

Of course I realise that not everyone is able to be choosey about the work they take on, and as Christians we must be aware of this. If you live in a depressed area of the country where jobs are hard to come by, you can only grab what you can. Many people just haven't been fortunate enough to have an education to get them beyond the factory floor. When wages are low, which is particularly the case with first jobs, the cost of living can make it just too expensive to accept posts.

Volunteer force
After I lost both FoE jobs, it was suggested that I work in their North London office as a volunteer. I was on the dole at the time, and there was then quite a restrictive limit on how many hours voluntary work you could do before you lost some of your benefit. And just the initial expense of travelling to and from the office − even if I could claim it back later − was prohibitively expensive. It just seemed out of the question. Some things you just have to let slip by.

But don't feel that as soon as you leave school you should necessarily go only for the nice career jobs. There are plenty of Christian organisations crying out for people to help them on, say, a one-year basis. Projects for the homeless, spiritual communities, overseas missions— all have short-term programmes. Check the classified ads in the Christian press, and for short-term work overseas, check out a copy of *Jobs Abroad* from the Christian Service Centre.[1]

It's quite common these days for young people with a place at a polytechnic or university to take a year out between school and study to travel, or do voluntary work, or just try out different things before they have to settle down at their desks. Whether or not you're going on to do any further education, why not take time out anyway to broaden your experiences, meet people, and give something back to the community. Get in touch with organisations like Careforce[2] or the Community Service Volunteers,[3] which have plenty of projects among disadvantaged people in this country.

If there's an organisation that you'd really like to work with − I recently read of a young English woman spending her year out working with Mother Theresa's team in Calcutta![4] − why not drop them a line and volunteer your services in return for bed and board. Or look at the needs among the people where you live and spend time working with the homeless, unemployed, addicts or handicapped.

At a Green level there are plenty of animal and bird sanctuaries, reserves and environmental projects that could do with an extra pair of hands. If you don't mind a bit of hard graft or office junior work and you've time to spare, then get moving. Who knows, it could lead on to more exciting programmes.

If you can't get a job, try and remain positive. Pray that God will show you what needs doing close to home. Are there neglected areas, rivers polluted with rubbish, places that with a bit of care could attract wildlife, or litter left lying around which would be more useful in a bottle or can bank?

Instead of moping around and getting apathetic, why don't you and your mates try and lift your spirits by taking responsibility for a part of your community. It will also keep you physically and mentally healthy and it's something you can put on your job application forms. When an interviewer asks you what you've been doing with yourself or what your interests are, you'll have a story to tell. In the meantime, you'll find yourself looking outwards and caring about the work that you're doing – and understanding its value in God's eyes.

Part-time practice

Part-time work can be useful whether you're in your mid-teens or older, though if it's an extra to full-time school work or a job, then do stop and consider why you're doing it. Certainly it's nice to have money to play with, but that's not the reason God gives it to us. He wants us to use it carefully and for His glory. Are we just doing the work for selfish reasons, or is there something more positive we can use it for?

In my time as a part-timer I've cleaned a church and

a restaurant, got the sack after three mornings of cleaning a supermarket, been a glass collector, a bar maid, a shop assistant and a library shelver. The restaurant cleaning was good for getting me up on summer days (6–9am); afterwards I'd cycle home for breakfast and was raring to go for the rest of the day. The bar work was good for the company. I recommend it for those old enough as an excellent way to get to know the locals if you've just moved into an area, and you will probably encounter far more respect for your Christian faith than you expect!

It was nice at the time to feel financially buoyant on the money I earned. It was not a lot, but I still recall the freedom I felt when for the first time I was able to buy a paperback book for a pound without having to worry about whether I'd have enough money left for other simple pleasures. And I could afford to buy decent birthday presents for my family at Christmas instead of scrimping around and ending up with cheap token gestures.

Incidentally, if you're soon to be a student, it's not always wise to get a reasonably well-paid job before you go off to study, unless you're a disciplined saver. You're likely to find your small student grant difficult to live on, whereas if you're not used to having money, then it could well seem like you're rich!

What are you going to do with your life?
Basically this work thing is about opening ourselves up to what God wants us to be. He gives us a joy of life, and with that joy He helps us enjoy work and play. Ideally, they should blend into each other, though there'll be times of trial in each. Stick close to God, and even the tough or dull moments will be revealed as part of His plan for you. And you'll find that not only does God use your interests and skills, but you'll be more willing to go where He wants you. Work doesn't have to be a nine-to-

five routine. God, in a very Green way, helps us to see and appreciate the work of our hands whatever we happen to be doing. And living for God becomes our life's work.

ACTION STATION

- Think about what you'd really like to do with your life, and make an attempt to do it! You might not be academic at school, but that doesn't mean you can't broaden your interests at home. And those are just as important in life as more formal education. If you need qualifications, you can always try and get them later.

- What do you do in your leisure time? It can give a strong indication of the type of person God has made you. Develop your talents and skills for God and you won't regret those abilities later on in life.

- Be ready to serve. Go out of your way to help others when they need it, and by doing it in God's name, He will take you further along His path.

11

Church Base

The Christian Church in the UK could and should be an ideal network of people living and worshipping together in an environment-friendly manner. What's more, the Green emphasis would be wholly Christian yet touch the local community and the wider world in a very clear and practical way.

Christian Ecology Link has begun the process. Its programme of 'Greening the Church' was launched in 1990 and it has a growing number of active local groups where Green Christians can get the support they need to help them bring Green thinking into their own churches.

In most churches there tends to be a small core group of committed people who seem to organise and get involved with much of what's going on in church life. They would certainly welcome another pair of hands, and if you get active, eventually they will take heed of what you want to say about the church going Green.

If the main body of the church seems reluctant to change its colour, don't give up. There should be a group within your church to suit you, whether it's for teenagers, singles, men, young wives, mothers and toddlers, with room for discussions and Bible study. It's here that your voice can be heard. Make sure to encourage others to get active too by suggesting particular activities for everyone to do.

If you're a teenager, have a word with your youth group/fellowship leader about what you'd like to see young people in your church covering as an issue and help them organise a programme. Tear Fund's *Third Track* magazine is a guide for youth leaders that will help here, and Scripture Union has plenty of materials that can be used with young people.

Anyone in their twenties who wants to get active in their church should be pounced on if the church has anything at all about it. At a number of churches I've been to I've found that on a first visit I only have to mention that I'm in editorial work as a profession, and I'm straightaway whisked off to meet the editor of the church paper. Which can sometimes be a drag. Not everybody wants to take what they do for a living during the week into their spare time hours, though I can understand why it's expected of you. I happen to be a qualified librarian, so I'd actually much rather help out on the bookstall, or reorganise the church library so people actually make use of it.

It's here that church members themselves as well as those who organise who does what should take a more Green approach to the distribution of jobs. Each of us has a range of talents and abilities, some of us have areas that need encouraging. If you think you'd like to have a go at helping out at something, whether it's flower arranging, tending the church grounds, looking after the children, welcoming newcomers or whatever, ask or turn up when volunteers are needed. Don't worry if you've never done anything like it before. A great deal of living is about learning. And you'll find that as you find a niche in church life, Church will become more important in your own life. You'll have found a place where you fit in.

Room for manoeuvre

Apart from the people who make up your church, probably the most important resource will be the sheer amount of space. This happens to be an important asset when recycling materials. One of the things that puts people off collecting newspapers, cans and similar things is that they have nowhere to put them. If you want to recycle papers then you'll need at least a ton's worth to get a decent payment from your local paper merchant.

Churches tend to be fairly large and airy buildings that make a lot of heating. See if your minister will allow you to block off an area to use to store materials for recycling. Or check if the church hall is available for, say, one day a month when you could ask everybody to bring their waste along – and make sure local non-churchgoers know about it too, by contacting the local paper with details.

Church halls are also valuable places for holding meetings to discuss different subjects or show films and get people thinking about the world's problems. Or join with your other church friends and start a club for local young children, especially if your community lacks facilities. Or hold a jumble sale (very Green!), and use the money you raise to support an environmental cause or development programme. Most charities will specify particular projects where money is needed if you write and ask. Why not contact organisations like Tear Fund, Traidcraft or Christian Aid and ask for information about the environmental projects they support in the Third World. Select one for the money you raise by jumble sales and recycling.

The Church has vital resources that should be shared with non-believers and attract them to what else goes on within its doors.

Among the church members themselves, suggest a 'share and share alike' scheme. God provides us with money and possessions not so that we hoard them and act as if what we own shows how valuable we are in His sight, but to share with other people. From those to whom much is given, much is expected. People with cars should give others lifts, people with babies share baby sitting, people with large houses and gardens invite hordes round for a church party, lend garden and DIY tools, share skills and talents. In some ways a church should be a self-sufficient community showing people how loving one another works in very practical ways – and how the strain on the world can be reduced by simply sharing what we have.

Real estate

Beyond the walls of many churches lie the church grounds or graveyard where wildlife can find a safe haven. Many are old and neglected, the ivy coverings on stone softening the hard edge of the tombs. In country villages they hold plant species that elsewhere might have been turned over in the soil. When seeds and pollen looking for a home fall on hallowed ground, they stand a far greater chance of living than when they fall on neighbouring fields and are overshadowed by the crops and ground down when they're harvested. In crowded towns and cities churchyards act as miniature nature reserves, and a network of green refuges.

Currently I live in a rambling old vicarage behind a church in West Hounslow. The church is in need of repair, but as I write there are at least four kestrels nesting in its eaves. One of my flatmates, Chris, works shifts and often leaves home at four in the morning. He's had his path crossed by a fox as he's walked out of our house on at least two occasions. And there's a feast of nettles to draw the red admirals.

A Green friend of mine tells me that whenever she sees grass or a fern poking out of a high brick wall, say on the side of a house, it brings a tear to her eye. She finds hope that despite all our bad treatment of the earth, and the way we flatten it and cover it in tarmac and concrete, nature soon finds a niche and clings on or crawls back. It doesn't take long to move back, and church grounds are places where it can rest in peace.

But the Church in this country – the state Church in particular — owns an awful lot of land. And though the Church of England stood for responsible stewardship long before Green thinking became generally fashionable, its Church Commissioners have been slow to adopt less intensive forms of farming and to halt hunting, though they aim to encourage wildlife conservation on Church farmland.

'What can all the Christian talk of love and mercy and compassion mean, if the Church (of England) is not going to lift a finger to prevent needless cruelty in its own backyard? What does it mean for the Church to speak so freely about responsible stewardship over nature, if, when it comes to it, the Church itself can find all kinds of good reasons for not exercising its own?'[1]

But there is certainly a move among church leaders to treat God's world with more respect. The latest Archbishop of Canterbury, George Carey, was hailed as the first Green Archbishop when his appointment was announced. The 1989 Baptist Union President, John Biggs, called for an active Christian concern for the environment during his year of office. He wrote two study booklets[2] looking at creation and worship in the light of the Christian faith. Find out from your minister or your denomination's own magazine or newspaper what projects your church could be following and how your denomination is going Green.

All part of the service
Many of the traditional church festivals are full of Green imagery. Originating in less industrialised times, the hymns, symbols and general atmosphere are of a less spoilt world. Harvest Festival is a good example, though 'We Plough the Fields and Scatter' is as relevant to farmers today as it's always been, despite their modern heavy machinery. One of my favourite hymns, 'There is a green hill . . .' has always conjured up images of a nicely curved mound of earth covered in green grass, when the reality must have been gruesomely different.

Maybe your church only has praise and worship books full of choruses rather than the traditional hymns. That's a shame. The church I grew up in still uses the English Hymnal, and most people there have probably never heard of Graham Kendrick. But I've learnt to appreciate the grand old hymns with their thrilling use of language and imagery. Whether your church sings choruses or hymns, flick your way through it and read the poetry of language that focuses on God's creation.

Why don't you and your friends work out a special Green service using the hymns you find as a starting point and filling the space in between with Bible readings, and pictures of creation drawn by the kindergarten, and act out one of Jesus' parables of the seeds or the lost sheep . . . Write too to your favourite Christian Third world or Green organisation and see if you can get somebody to speak to your church or fellowship group as well.

These days it's traditional to serve cups of coffee and tea for churchgoers after the service so that they can meet each other. Serving the refreshments is often regarded as a woman's job, while the men might not even be asked. Why don't you and your friends, whatever their sex, help out on a regular basis. Stock up on 'right-on' tea and coffee from Third World charities, and put up posters and leave out leaflets so that people can see what drinking these drinks means to people in the Third World.

If the hot drinks are always served in those flaky polystyrene cups, show that money and resources can be saved by asking people to give you their old mugs or cups and saucers (most people have some gathering dust at the back of their kitchen cupboards or can at least spare one) and use those instead. And afterwards have an 'all hands on deck' session washing them up — and remember to use a friendly washing-up liquid like Ecover or Ark.

As well as the church bookstall, your church will probably have a small library. Often these are neglected and the books become out-of-date, though some books do stand the test of time but are just not known about. Take responsibility for the library — though ask your minster first — and ask people to hand over any Christian books they've finished with so that others can read them too. Look out for others in charity shops and at jumble sales. Encourage use of the library by writing book reviews for your church paper.

Because of your interest in a Christian approach to Green matters and your respect for God's creation, you may find yourself attracted to Creation Festivals and Services at major churches and cathedrals across the UK. But be careful. Many are in fact multi-faith celebrations, where representatives of the world's faiths gather together to worship and thank God for his creation and celebrate the earth. And the name of Jesus is often conspicuous by its absence.

A Bible-based Christianity believes that when Jesus said 'I am the Way, the Truth and the Life, no-one comes to the Father except through me,'[3] He actually meant it, and that belief doesn't fit into a multi-faith worship environment. Even when services claim to be Christian, there can be too much of an emphasis on the Creation itself as if it is only by treating it better, being in harmony with it, that everything will turn out all right.

Yet this denies God's intervention into our history following *our* downfall. It ignores the fact that salvation for the world and hope for our futures come only through the life, death and resurrection of Jesus Christ.

ACTION STATION

- Think of what you can share with your church, whether it's time, talents or things you own. Volunteer these services through the church noticeboard or newsletter.

- Suggest a tidy up session of the church grounds. Plants need pruning, grass needs cutting, rubbish and dead wood need to be cleared away so that new life can thrive. Get everybody involved, whatever their age and abilities.

- Ask around to find out if there are any other Green Christians in your church. Get a group going so that there's more chance of your plans being achieved.

12

Travelling Light

Each one of us has to get from A to B and back again
in our day-to-day lives. And whether we're going to
school or church, visiting friends or just going 'out', the
type of transport we use to get us there affects the
environment and our relationship with other people in
our community.

It's not easy looking at transport from a Christian
viewpoint. The choice of transport in Bible times was
far more limited than it is now. People either travelled
on foot, or went by cart, animal or boat depending on
the distance to be covered and a person's wealth. And
each type of transport made little impact on the
environment.

However, the *way* people travelled 2,000 or so years
ago can still direct our journeys in today's mobile world.
Christ and his disciples walked most of the time, but Jesus
also rode on a donkey and went by boat too. What is
clear about His journeys is that He was rarely far from
ordinary people. For the woman who had suffered
bleeding for twelve years, Jesus was literally at arm's
length; she reached out and touched Him as He passed
her by, and she was healed.[1] Jesus' triumphant entry
into Jerusalem was on a humble donkey[2] rather than a
lofty camel or proud warhorse.

Today, God doesn't want us going *everywhere* by
shanks's pony or by horse power just to prove the point;
we live in the modern world where time and convenience
do matter. But as Christians we should consider how our
choice of transport affects the environment and our
relationships with other people before we set off on our

107

travels. Often there is a distinct connection between the two.

Foot soldiers

'Everything is within walking distance if you've got the time,' American comic Steve Wright has said. And he has a point. One of the things which struck me while watching the epic stage presentation of Dickens' *Nicholas Nickleby* was that during the last century, people actually used to walk from York to London. These days, people too used to car travel have difficulty even thinking about footing it, whatever the distance.

Which is a shame, because walking is healthy, relaxing, sociable, cheap and essentially pollution-free, and can be done by people of all ages. Nor do you have to be tremendously fit or spend an awful lot on sports gear before you can start doing it.

On short journeys be sure to use your feet. Instead of having to concentrate on the road in front of you as you must do when you're driving, you can relax. And not only is walking less stressful, but you save money by not using car parks and petrol − and you're helping the environment too. Get off before a fare stage if you're going by bus or train and use the money you save for a more worthy cause.

Walking gives you a breathing space in your day, a chance to wind down and think and pray. With your feet on the ground you get a better view of where you live, you meet people, and you can stop and chat. And you notice the little things around you and understand your community better.

In theory, walking is pollution-free provided you take your litter home with you. However, people do leave their tracks behind, and popular routes such as coastal paths have been badly eroded. Elsewhere, rare wild flowers have been trampled underfoot and grassways left barren. So there is a need for care, though to put it in perspective, you only have to walk along the Ridgeway long-distance path that stretches from Avebury stone circle to Ivinghoe to see the far worse havoc caused to the countryside by motorbikes and cars.

Jesus' willingness to walk alongside people is something Christian walkers should bear in mind today. The very art of walking, whether it's along a street, on a hike or in the local park, involves people altering their speed as they feel fit, and falling into line with others. Sure, there's nothing wrong with walking on your own, it's a time when you can feel very close to God. But if you're walking in a group, you can end up speaking to different people and forging new friendships as your own speed ebbs and flows. It's about making sure no one is left behind.

Walking to school is a great way of getting to know children from other school years – and from other schools. And with the increasing reports of child abductions, it's a way of looking after the more vulnerable and shy members of your school who might otherwise go home alone.

Make sure you walk to church with your friends or family each quiet Sunday morning. Unless you live far from anywhere, are physically unable to get to church on foot, or your parents ferry elderly people to services in the family car, then there's really no reason to use a car to get to church. If you still do, then you need to ask yourself why you're not going to a more local one.

The sight of people walking from different directions and congregating at a church is a very strong statement in a society where most people don't go to church and many on a Sunday morning are out mowing the front lawn or cleaning the car.

You and your Christian friends could go for a prayer walk and ask God to open your eyes not only to the sufferings and joys of the people you live among, but also to the wonders of and damage to your surroundings, whether you're on a nature trek or a wander along a city's crowded streets.

Getting your skates on

There's a theory that the reason the Daleks didn't take over the world in those old Doctor Who series is that they could never manage stairs . . . Skateboards and roller

skates do best on smooth surfaces too, but are portable enough for you to overcome not only stairs, but pavement obstacles and grass verges as well. With confidence, you can swerve round and jump over them too.

They're a speedy, efficient and environment-friendly way to get around. But be sure to take care of others using the same pathways. It can be quite frightening to walk along the street and suddenly be approached by a gang of young people on wheels. But it can be exciting to see how fast you can go. On the plus side, both roller skates and skate boards are far quicker than walking, don't need parking space and are a great way to travel both short and long distances.

Pedal power

There's something about cycling. Rattling along with friends, laughing and singing at the top of your voice as you race each other furiously on a summer's afternoon like something out of *The Sound of Music*. Getting home from work or studies *fast*. But, warns Karen Christensen in her book *Home Ecology*: 'There's no doubt that the main problem for a cyclist is the sheer mass of metal which threatens you every time you venture out, and in a collision the cyclist is always the one at risk. Many car drivers behave appallingly to cyclists, while most are simply oblivious of us (the few who are courteous are probably cyclists themselves).

'Nevertheless, cycling is a convenient, efficient and enjoyable way to get around – much faster than walking or rush hour driving, and eminently suited to short journeys. While weather is sometimes a problem, safety is the most important deterrent for most people.'[3]

Surprisingly, though, cycling can be just as efficient in a built-up city as along a quiet country road. One of my best bicycle buys was *On your Bike*.[4] This is basically a collection of A-Z style maps of Central London, with cycle routes marked by red lines. This booklet has guided me and my 'trusty steed' across the capital's leafy parks, around quiet squares and along quaint backstreets. It's helped me avoid dangerous main roads so that I reached my destination safely, *and* showed me a slice of London I would otherwise have missed.

It's easy to work out your own bike routes for the area in which you live. Buy a cheap local map and mark out cycle ways – remember to include council cycle paths – which help you get around town while avoiding dangerous traffic. And do trial runs to test out your routes.

Cycling this way helps you appreciate a district, its people, its architecture; you gain a sense of community. God helps you see the wonders around you from your saddle. And when it's just you and your two-wheeler humming along, He can help you focus your thoughts on Him. Cycling provides you with good thinking and praying time, particularly when you're in an area you're very familiar with. I once spent a five-mile cycle ride from the centre of Manchester to my home singing and praising God in a rather tuneless but totally non-stop and spontaneous way.

Because bikes are so relatively easy to use — and easy to park (though do get yourself a good strong padlock to secure it) — you soon find that once laborious journeys on foot or by public transport or car become a pleasure. You're more mobile so you cycle round to friends who live a few miles away, and more willing to do errands for family and friends because it now takes a fraction of the time. It's less of a trial to go the extra mile . . .

I've found, too, that having to lift my bike up and down stairs, particularly on railway stations, has made me far more aware of the problems faced by people in wheelchairs or with prams and pushchairs — and so more ready to help them.

Motorbikin'

Symbol of teen rebellion, the motorbike is also a high-powered way of zipping along roads. Many parents fear the day that their adolescents decide they want a bike because of the dangers involved in negotiating traffic. So if your parents are reluctant to let you have one, don't knock them; it's because they're concerned for your safety.

In Scotland, bikers must now be trained before they can go on the road. That's no bad thing. Bikes have a tremendous power within them and with no real barrier between you and the road or the traffic, you can be very vulnerable. It's important to wear the proper gear of leather boots, gloves, a jacket, and above all a helmet — they're all designed to keep you in one piece should you and your bike part company mid-ride.

Like push bikes, motorbikes and mopeds can twist through traffic jams and are easy to park. But, declared

Motorbike International editor Tom Isitt: 'If you are concerned about the environment, if you would like to see a more pleasant earth, get rid of your motorbike. It's as simple as that.

'The internal combustion engine is ecologically unsound, and that's all there is to it. Every time you start up your bike you begin to pump carbon monoxide, nitrogen oxides, hydrocarbons and lead into the atmosphere. You are contributing to a problem that is slowly and inexorably choking the earth.'[5] There's nothing like setting the record straight.

Nevertheless, if you still want to bike it after reading all that, be heartened that the motorbike is Greener than other vehicles powered by the internal combustion engine. It's more fuel efficient than cars. And nine in ten bikes can use unleaded petrol without having to be altered in any way.[6] But because the engine becomes less efficient, other dangerous pollutants are pumped out instead.

But don't despair. Parts of your bike and its waste can be recycled. It is illegal to pour waste oil down drains. Instead take it along to your local civil amenity site (number in the phone book alongside local council services) to be recycled. Batteries too. It's not so easy to get rid of dangerous waste like brake fluid and anti-freeze, and if you can't find a safe place, Isitt advises that you pour it down a household drain where it will be treated at a sewage works rather than a roadside drain where it will run into the nearest river.

Car trouble

From a Green viewpoint, it's very easy to dismiss cars as a means of transport. 'Although the car means a great deal to the national economy and to the individuals who own them there is little doubt that, despite its many conveniences, its vast cost in social, economic and environmental terms is destroying our communities, our land, our resources, our atmosphere and our very lives,'

113

says Jonathon Holliman in the *Consumer's Guide to the Protection of the Environment.* 'It is both a symptom and a cause of a large proportion of the environmental diseases we see around us every day, and it has become one of the most powerful tools of psychological manipulation and consumer enslavement ever devised.'[7]

That's a damning statement, but although as Christians we must take all this into account, we must recognise too that motor vehicles have their uses. In the event of an emergency, they are often vital in saving time and lives. As a child I once gashed my leg badly in a fall. We had no family car, but my mother and I were ferried by our neighbour to the local hospital. And though I don't drive, I am always grateful when moving house for the readiness of close friends to use their cars to shift my junk. I don't know what I'd do without them.

However, in our daily travels, we need to ask ourselves if our car journey is really necessary, and whether we'd be better off walking or using a more public type of transport. Cars by their very nature and size tend to isolate people. They keep the family in a secure and compact unit, and though they emphasise family ties, at the same time they leave people on the outside looking in. When Gary Numan sang 'Here in my car, I feel safest of all, I can lock all my doors, it's the only way to live,'[8] he expressed not only the security but also the separation that the 'metal box' brings.

Admittedly, in America in particular the car is a key to a fast social life. Drive-in movies, cruising down the city's main street — it's all part of the culture. In some US cities, anybody walking on the sidewalk is considered a bit strange. In this country, it's very different. Approximately four out of ten households still do not have cars. So, if you are fortunate enough to be driven to school and on awaydays, consider people you know who cannot get to places so easily and offer them a lift. In parts of the States, car-sharing is encouraged by having lanes reserved on the freeway for cars carrying more than one passenger.

You may already have a car, or at least be determined to get your own as soon as it's legal for you to drive. A car certainly provides independence – but be careful that the freedom it might bring to you and your passengers doesn't turn into a determination to hold onto your rights as owner of the vehicle. I vividly recall a 'night on the town' courtesy of the first driver in my group of close friends. As one by one the rest of us began to flag and drift from the dance floor, she, her eye on some lad, doggedly kept bopping 'til the night's end. By then, the rest of us were bored and would rather have been in bed.

If you want to carry your friends, do fix safety belts in the back as well as the front seats. Anybody under 14 must by law be belted up, but it's a good idea if you enable your passengers whatever their age to be more safe. Without belts, in the event of a serious crash, not only will the back-seat passengers be flung forward through the windscreen, but they'll hit the front-seat passengers and cause serious injury to them too on the way there. Cars are potentially very dangerous weapons and you must bear this in mind when you're on the road.

As Christians, we must also think about what we're saying through our vehicle. It's very tempting to go for the most flashy vehicle or the one with most power, but we must be careful that we don't cause others to be jealous of our possessions. A well-off friend of mine treated himself to £10,000 worth of glossy Ford Escort. But he soon became guiltily aware that his less well-paid work-mate was suitably impressed and thinking of buying one himself, even though he couldn't really afford it.

If we have chosen to own a nice car, then we must be willing to share it and use it to glorify God. We need to do all in our power to reduce its impact on the world by running it on unleaded petrol and using it less. And it's best if the car's second-hand. According to Greenpeace figures, 6,000 new cars take to Britain's already congested roads every day, adding to the 21 million cars we already own.[9]

Jonathon Holliman advises: 'When you buy a car, look at what you are buying — not in the advertiser's terms but in your own. Until the car ceases to be a status symbol (an idea carefully nurtured by car manufacturers' advertising), people will continue to buy much bigger and more powerful cars than they need or want. The more 'car' you buy, the more you pollute.'[10]

Next time you're standing in a bus queue, count how many cars go by containing only the driver. Divide by four and just think of all the space, quietness, fresher air, and safer streets there'd be if car drivers nationwide filled their cars with people going in the same direction, to the same school, shopping centre or workplace.

Ask yourself if you could do without your car. How many of your journeys could not be accomplished by other means? It is an essential, or a luxury for your leisure moments? If you find it hard to make your money go around, don't scrimp and save on little things which will have hardly any effect. Think big, think drastically, and swap your four wheels for two.

Cars are the biggest single consumer of world resources, and a major source of environmental pollution.[11] If we want to protect God's world from environmental ruin, then we'd do well to go a different way.

Plane sailing
Living on an island, the only way to get away is by air or sea. Any journey within Britain shouldn't warrant a flight, though business people will justify it as a great time saver.

When I used to return to my parents' London home from Manchester for the student holidays, I always phoned from Euston Station to warn them that I'd be at their place in about an hour's time. It took less than that to fly from Manchester to London's Heathrow Airport, and though I never did as I could never afford to, it would have been fun to phone from Manch and give them the same warning.

But our nation's air space is dangerously packed and sooner or later there's going to be a mid-air collision. By using planes for short journeys we are giving our vote to the introduction of more and more planes. If you're going to the close continent you have a choice between boat or plane. Boats take far longer and there's a long car or train journey at the other end. Planes get you to the heart of a country, but you experience less of it though on a clear day you'll get a panoramic view. Planes also drop their fuel in mid-air before landing and so pollute the surrounding countryside.

Whether boating or flying, do go easy on the duty free. It can be very tempting if you've got a lot of spare money, but the environmental impact of a boat or plane carrying that extra cargo is heavy. More fuel is needed to ferry all those bottles. Think about it long enough and you'll realise that the whole idea behind duty free goods is absurd. Totally unnecessary, already overpriced products are bought as you're leaving a country. You take them up in the air with the only purpose of bringing them down again.

If you don't think about what you're doing you could buy products that actually travel to and from a destination for no reason whatsoever other than to save a few quid. It's a very selfish way of shopping when you realise the cost of transporting all that drink and perfume across the world. If you do have any spare cash at the end of your foreign hols, change the notes back into sterling or keep them as souvenirs. Better still, deposit them and any coins in the charity boxes they have at some airports or give them to The Children's Society or your local Oxfam shop.

Going public
If Jesus and his disciples and their entourage were around
today, would they be like some rock band or football
team travelling from town to town in a tourbus? I doubt
it. I can't imagine the lads and their womenfolk peering
down from coach windows at their supporters banging
on the metal sides – with no proper way of communicating. I'd expect them instead to pour into a tube
train compartment, touching people's lives.

Jesus went where the people were. Today, people are
crammed into buses and trains. They're as public a place
as a busy city street, and it's up to us to make an effort
to home in on these people's needs, to talk to them rather
than cutting ourselves off behind a newspaper or book.

God does sit us opposite or next to particular people
for a reason. He shows us our common humanity in a
public vehicle. Once travelling in Kenya on a *matatu* bus
– basically a privately-run minibus service of vehicles
practically stuck together with sellotape and generally
crammed full with people – I got talking to two Kenyans.
I was the only white person on board, and finding out
that I was British they wanted to discuss our government's
approach to South Africa! At the time I was squashed
into a corner of the van, and somebody's elbow was
sticking into me and I could hardly move my head . . .
and they told me that they looked to Britain because of
our history in abolishing the slave trade, which I'd never
heard before.

Also in Kenya, on a thirteen-hour overnight train
journey from Mombassa to Nairobi, I spent hours sitting
in the corridor when I had a bed to go to, talking to a
guy who'd just spent months working with Bill 'Born
Free' Adamson, and who had the photos of Bill and the
lions to prove it. It was a fascinating journey.

Travelling by public transport, we're travelling in a
smaller version of the world, cut off in a sense from
everything outside, but sharing our space with people of

different backgrounds, races, ages and experiences. There are moments when everybody shares a joke, a moment together.

British Rail guards have a line in tannoy patter that can have a train of passengers in stitches, intentionally or otherwise. And I was once weaving down the aisle of a Manchester-London train trying not to spill my coffee over somebody's lap when I spotted Bobby Charlton coming down the aisle towards me. As I shifted out of the way, I could see fathers down the length of the compartment pointing him out to their young sons. It was a moment for smiles all round and quite unforgettable.

During a train or bus journey, we experience a smaller kind of world. Our planet has been nicknamed 'Spaceship Earth' — in its most basic form, it's a massive Starship Enterprise with all our physical needs on board. But the world is really too big for us to think of it in those terms. If when going public we try to think about the planet as if it's the bus we're in — and that we're all in the same boat — we begin to understand that if we carelessly waste the things on board we're going to run out. There's limit to the oil and metal, and we need to divide up our food and drink if everybody is to last the long journey . . .

Travelling by rail is probably the best way to see a country. Instead of being caught on motorways, you're literally flying at ground level with a clear view that can stretch for miles. Not only do you see the range of places that people call 'home', but the character and extent of the countryside too.

David Cohen, Scripture Union's General Director for England and Wales, calls the times spent looking out of trains 'little bits of celebration'. It's a chance to take a breather and appreciate the marvellous view of God's world. 'I have lots of breaks within a work programme. While travelling, a train journey becomes a break. I enjoy looking out at the countryside without feeling I'm wasting time. I make space.'[12]

We gain a wider vision of a country's landscape and its valleys, folds and plains. Though Britain with its population of 56 million is a crowded country, I am very heartened by the amount of stretches of relatively unspoilt land I've seen from train windows.

Supporting public transport is a way of keeping it like that. Friends of the Earth (FoE) believes the future of transport has to be public. The alternative is a country covered with tarmac to cater for the car. 'Road building and road widening across London requires the destruction of thousands of homes and numerous parks and green spaces,' FoE declared in a leaflet calling for an end to massive road-building in the capital, but which applies just as easily to the rest of the nation. 'Roads will also generate more traffic and more pollution, damaging human health and helping to destroy the global environment.'

We can't afford to let the car get its way. As Christians we must travel with a respect for other people, for the landscape and for the atmosphere which God created. Going public means not only living life alongside other people in a most day-to-day way, but travelling in a way that drastically cuts down our impact on the world.

ACTION STATION

- If you own a car and when ferrying friends around aren't keen on asking them to share petrol costs, get your friends to contribute some money to your favourite cause instead.

- Pluck up courage to start talking to the person you sit next to on the bus or train. And whether you've a neighbour or not, see how far you can travel without using your walkman . . .

- Broaden your horizons. Even if you already travel Greenly, try another kind of travel. Be prepared to make use of a combination of vehicles to get from A to B.

- Get yourself a good pair of leather walking shoes or boots (don't believe the so-called 'experts' – you can pick up a pair for less than £30, less than £20 if you've small feet), make yourself a packed lunch, take some money for the ride home, and start walking. You'll be surprised at how far you'll get.

13

Free Time

Our time is not our own. There are lots of pressures on our leisure time from school, family, and church. Depending on our age, there's homework to be done, chores and responsibilities in the home and church services and meetings to attend. And ultimately all our time belongs to God – so we must use it wisely.

In the film *Blade Runner* the dying android sinisterly but movingly played by Rutger Hauer declares to onlooker Harrison Ford that 'time is lost like a tear in the rain'. It's a beautiful and true thought. Time is washed away. Blink, and you miss it. So we must be careful and constructive with our free time.

The most important thing to try and do each day is to spend some of it in a quiet place with God and His Word. Reading the Bible helps you to be on the right wavelength with life. You approach day-to-day living more calmly and see everything from a new perspective. You come to understand which are life's important issues and which are simply trivial and not worth worrying about.

In a Green sense you become more confident about your responsibilities towards God's planet and see the world as if you're standing back from it. You find it easier to recognise the knock-on effect our actions make, *and* enjoy your place within the world.

Then when it comes to using your leisure time you're more geared to using it Greenly and for God.

Time limit
We live in such a fast-paced and packed-with-activity

world that many people have to make special time for a moment for themselves – or anyone else, come to that.

But leisure time is important not just because it gives us space to stop, look and listen and recharge our batteries and is vital to our mental, physical and spiritual health. It also helps us think properly and get our priorities right regarding our relationships with other people and with God and the world. It's about having time to give.

A friend indeed

Friendship is tremendously important and good friends take time to cultivate. The way to test your compatibility is to see whether after years out of touch you start from where you left off, but there needs to be a strong foundation.

Put yourself out for other people. Make yourself available. And don't dismiss the quiet ones and the ones who aren't popular. I've often found that it's the apparently shy people who are far more interesting than the 'life and soul of the party' types. It's almost as if the quiet people beaver on quietly with their lives without other people noticing unless they take the trouble to ask. You can have some fascinating conversations with them. And the ones that everybody can't stand are rarely as bad as they're painted. With some unfortunate people a rumour has spread around them over the years that is terribly difficult to shake off. Ask God to remove your blinkers and help you see these people as He sees them and reach out to them as He would.

Pop round and visit people or get in touch by mail or phone. Maybe you've been out of touch with old friends for a number of years, and the gap in time now seems too vast to bridge. Take a chance and contact them anyway. Chances are you'll be pleasantly surprised.

People from my secondary school year now try and meet up informally on an annual basis. So far we've managed it twice at north-west London pubs. And it's amazing how little people actually change. Certainly everybody seems to have grown a bit as people, their characters have branched out, but they're still basically the same. The once very shy ones have come out of their shells, but they're the same personalities. And so you find yourself chatting away to somebody you haven't seen for eight or ten years. Interestingly, too, the barriers that had built up around the different factions in the classroom when we were at school now crumble away, and you end up having lengthy conversations with people you barely smiled at across the desks. I recall talking to Rosemarie after ten years and asking what she was doing now. She recounted how after leaving school she'd worked for a while in her father's shop but got to the point where she wanted a change. 'This might sound strange,' she said, 'but I just prayed to God to give me an idea of what to do. And I suddenly thought of being a nurse.' And that is exactly what she did.

At the time of writing, I'm gearing myself up for The 'long time, no see, just because I haven't been in touch doesn't mean I haven't been thinking of you, now that I'm living in a big place it seems a shame not to invite people round, and as it's my twenty-seventh birthday it's a good time to have a' Party. I've invited practically everybody who's in my address book, regardless of how long it is since I last saw them. And though not everybody can come, the phone calls, postcards and letters I have received to tell me yea or nay have turned out to be just as important to me. Old acquaintances have proved that they don't forget, and friendships have been rekindled. The years simply melt away.

Friendship is a cheap way of spending your leisure time, though once you get involved with friends' problems it becomes more expensive in terms of the greater time you spend caring and being there when they need you. But at the same time, your friendship becomes deeper and more rewarding for it.

But don't just check up on friends your own age. Go and visit older people who live in your street. Many are single and don't see many people in their day-to-day lives, yet they have extraordinary stories to tell of ordinary people's lives. If they've lived in the area for a long time, they'll remember what it was like before many of the present buildings sprouted. They'll have lived through at least one world war and have seen the changes of many decades. The twentieth century has developed at a rapid pace, and people have lived through some jarring changes that the vast majority of people in time and in today's world have never had to deal with. Ask these friends about their jobs, what school life was like for them, and what they did in their spare time. You'll both enjoy the company.

Visit old people's homes, too. People here often feel neglected by the world outside, and private homes in particular miss the visits from local schools and church groups. It can take a lot to remain positive as what Americans term 'a shut-in' and you can bring a breath of fresh air and a change of scene into their lives.

Friendship is both Christian and Green. It puts value on people, is a simple human need fulfilled, and is cheap and doesn't need a lot of energy or resources to keep a good relationship going. It's basic human action and it's free!

Rhythm and greens

If we've been leading a hectic life, we need time just to recharge our batteries, to slow down. It might sound dull, but I find that the rhythm of ironing and other household chores gets me back into the right gear. It's restful, pretty mindless and it just makes a break in the day while I'm doing something that needs doing.

I'm a pretty disorganised kinda person, and so if I find that I've got time to do such basic activities − which for me are non-essentials − it means that it really is a true break, and I savour the moment. Repairing, polishing and just being practical at a very low-key level – when I find time to do them – are things I can quietly enjoy. For me these are moments when I am able to appreciate silence and simple pleasures in God's company.

Letter-writing too has a similar impact, though your thoughts are more focused on your friend and your own news. A good detailed letter can take an hour or so to write, but once you get into doing it it's a pleasure both to give and to receive. After all, handwritten envelopes promise so much more than formal typed official notes. Once you start writing you get to recognise who your letters are from before you've opened the envelope. My sis Jane has distinctive writing and her letters are fun, so that when the post hits the mat, I instantly know she's written and it immediately brings a smile to my face. During 1990's scorching July she sent me a postcard showing a couple of Emperor penguins on the Antarctic ice. On the back of the card she'd scrawled, 'Bluddy hot, innit.' I had to laugh.

Sometimes you remember a friend from the past, or you hear of someone you know who's been bereaved. Drop them a line to let them know you're thinking of them. The post is still very powerful. If there's something that bugs you politically write to your MP, ask how he or she is responding to particular issues. Use your local paper's letters page to draw readers' attention to environmental activities whether positive or negative in your neighbourhood. Join Amnesty International and write to prisoners of conscience and their captors to push for release. Jubilee Campaign which focuses on cases of persecuted Christians across the world encourages supporters to pray – and write where practical to those imprisoned for their faith. If there's a restriction on letters, send postcards instead to help bring colour into their cells, and the knowledge that people on the outside care.

Use recycled paper and envelopes for all this letter-writing. And get into the routine of sorting your waste into different materials for the different destinations whether it's can bank, school or charity shop. Time-consuming it can turn out to be, but at the same time you're involved in an important activity, yet taking it slow. Combine your journeys of waste delivery with shopping, visiting friends or going to work or school, or take a Saturday morning to clear the lot from your home in one go.

Use your time thoughtfully. It's one of the most precious resources God has given us. It's not for us to squander, but to aim to use to its full potential.

ACTION STATION

- Read:
  Leisure by Fred Martin and Aubrey Whittle (Hutchinson, 1982).

- By focusing on God, it's amazing how everything falls into place and you seem to make better use of your time. Pray that God will help you use the time He's given you for His glory.

- If major things need to be done, do them now. Otherwise you'll only find that other less important activities push them out. And you soon find yourself doing anything but the most important.

- Contact the headquarters of your favourite Green organisation to find out the address of your local group, and get involved. Volunteer your services at the meetings. Don't just sit there, but join in the action too.

- Keep a good sense of humour. Enjoy the world around you. Be impulsive now and then. Never lose your youthfulness.

14

Away From It All

When we're ready for a break, it's very tempting to leave our consciences at home while we go off and enjoy ourselves. But being a Christian means that we shouldn't switch off our faith when we feel like it. The way we see the world, highlighted by the Holy Spirit, means that we must take our beliefs into account when we're deciding where to holiday, too. Our beliefs should shape our reasons for going there.

Beach combing
From an early age the vast majority of British kids are taken off to the seaside for their holidays. Beaches are a very cheap way to spend the day.

For years we've had to watch out for patches of oil and the odd decomposing seagull or jellyfish, but our coastline and coastal waters are increasingly threatened by pollution from untreated sewage and coastal industries. Teenage swimmers and watersporters like surfers and waterskiers are more at risk from contaminated water simply because they tend to spend more time in the sea and swallow polluted water. These days you just can't be sure whether it's healthy to go for a dip or dig sand pits. The image of Britain's glorious stretching bays is tarnished.

It's a great shame as the UK has enormous potential for holidaying despite our unsure weather. If you must go down to the sea again — and why not — do be sure to take your litter home with you. And watch out for that left by others. One hot summer day which brings out the crowds has a devastating impact on the amount of rubbish that goes into the sea.

Going Green

My sister Jane and I once spent an enjoyable evening stroll with our parents along Newquay's long bay which is broken into a string of coves. The tide was out and there was hardly anyone else on the sands. But dotted everywhere, over rocks, on the shore, by crumbling sand castles were drink cans. The two of us picked up a few, but before long it became a litter-clearing fury. We found a couple of plastic bags and crammed the cans into those, but there were just too many for us to carry. Cove upon cove was full of this litter, just waiting to be washed out to sea. Our action didn't make a massive impact, but it was important to us. If you live on the coast, why not get a gang of like-minded friends together and have a regular evening clear-up. Take the cans along to your local can bank, or collect them to raise money for charity.

It's not just the beaches that are at risk from holidaymakers. Cliffs and coastal land are threatened not only by the wear and tear of visitors, but by the building of caravan parks, hotels and leisure facilities, too. There are limits. Since 1965, the National Trust's Enterprise Neptune has worked to acquire 900 miles of beautiful and vulnerable coastline around England, Wales and Northern Ireland. Certainly enjoy the views from above, but tread carefully.

Getting active

All young people get to the point where they want to branch out on their own with their friends. But where to go, and what to do? There are plenty of cheap Green and Christian holidays that aren't about spending a week lazing around but instead being active while enjoying yourself at the same time.

I spent a week's holiday over the summer between my sixth form years coppicing with the British Trust for Conservation Volunteers (BTCV) near Diss in Suffolk. It was fun, tiring, practically cured my fear of spiders, helped me identify a number of trees and introduced me to a group of people from a variety of backgrounds, ages and nationalities. You can also have a go at dry-stone walling, clearing out lakes and protecting reserves as well as plenty of other conservation jobs. The BTCV also has weekend 'tasks' but as these mean you must, by their nature, miss church on Sunday, it's not wise to go on too many of these. The 'back to the land' aspect of the BTCV is very rewarding. You learn age-old skills of protecting and nurturing a local environment that you take with you into the future.

There are plenty of volunteer 'get stuck in' jobs going during your summer holidays and over Christmas. I found a week helping out with Crisis at Christmas's refuge for the homeless thoroughly enjoyable for the hard work and the company. I was at my parents' home for Christmas Day and at my mother's church was asked whether I'd have preferred helping the homeless to spending Christmas Day with my folks. It was a difficult question.

Get yourself a copy of the *International Directory of Voluntary Work*.[1] Your local library should have a copy or similar to help you plan your time away. Or pop into your local Christian bookshop for various Christian magazines and check the listings for things to do and organisations to contact.

If you want a time of travelling from A to B to C to D, then join the Youth Hostel Association which as well as having a wide range of activities to suit all tastes – sport, outdoor pursuits, crafts, nature watching – acts as a cheap way to see the countryside while being based in some fascinating buildings including a castle, coastal mills, rambling beamed cottages and fine houses.

Home and away

Not everybody can get away for a break, and few spend the whole of their summer holidays away from home. Remember how as a child you used to play with the kids across the road from you or in the next garden? You'd wander round each other's houses and fill those long summer days with simple pleasures.

As you get older, you want to be doing a bit more. The London Borough where I grew up – Hillingdon – would put on a range of activities every summer for the area's young people. For a number of years the four of us would bus up to Ruislip Lido to canoe. Maybe your council runs a similar programme. Check at your local library for details, and see if there are any summer schools in practical work that might suit you too.

Why don't you and some friends explore the area where you live? Pick up a map and go to all those places that you've never been to though they're within a few miles of where you live. Act the tourist. If there's a Tourist Information Office close to home, pop in and pick up plenty of leaflets on what's on. Join a guided tour. Visit museums, however small. Wander through parks and gardens. Tread quietly into churches. It helps you appreciate the place where you live. Walk down your local High Street and look above the shopline at the sheer variety of architecture.

In my late teens I began to tire of the north-west London region where I'd been born and brought up. It was great when we were children because there was plenty of green space to play about in, a brook to wade in and search for tadpoles, and it was safe so the local children could go off and explore on their own. But as I got older I got more and more disillusioned with the place. Being a London suburb, it seemed neither one thing nor the other. The local theatres showed dreadful bedroom farces and the cinemas, what remained of them, were three-in-ones and tended to screen blockbusters. If you wanted quality or to go and see a good band, you had to travel on the tube into Town. And after a while, that just became a drag.

But, I don't know why, my views of the place have

mellowed over the years. I've grown fond of it. It's what the poet John Betjeman called Metroland, out on the Underground's Uxbridge line. The architecture is classic 1930s – from the houses, to the local railway stations, to the shopping streets. Rayners Lane, with its art deco cinema – unfortunately being taken apart – has a marvellous sweeping curve down its main street. Eastcote Station, until they took out the old ticket office in a fit of London Transport modernisation, was a living museum piece. I love the softened edges of the buildings of that era and the human scale of everything. Now, I can quite happily wander along its streets appreciating the atmosphere and style of the area.

Check out the local history department of your local library and see what you can find out about the place where you live. So few people do look closely at their day-to-day surroundings, that you'll find a real enthusiasm for what you discover which you'll want to share.

Breakaway

But do try and spend some time, however short, away from home, particularly if your holiday is stretching out over the summer. Sometimes you just need a change of scene. It's nice to visit relatives in far-off places or friends in other towns. If you've a good bike, cycle out to a neighbouring town or village and enjoy the break. If you or one of your good friends owns a car, why not suggest you all pile in and drive to a seaside resort.

My group of close friends – we've known each other since our schooldays – plus boyfriends crammed into Naomi and Chris's camper van and set off from north-west London to the coast to visit our other good friend Claire and her bloke Michael in Worthing. It was Claire's birthday and she had no idea that we were planning to descend on her home. The whole thing was very impromptu. We all had a great time, and we made it home in a day.

Whether for a day or the whole weekend, that sort of trip away can be as good a break from routine as a week away. Because your time is short, you not only learn to pack all you need into a small holdall, but you manage to cram as many things into your day as possible, or take it leisurely if you please. Either way recharges your batteries. And getting into the habit of taking short breaks now prepares you for working life when holidays are fairly limited and breaks from work and home duties are just as important.

In a far country

Stepping onto the soil of a foreign country we should carry our Christian faith with us as readily as our holiday gear. As Christians concerned about the wider world, however we holiday it's important that we keep our eyes and ears open to our new surroundings. It's the easiest thing to do to switch off and play the absolute tourist with no thought for the impact the tourist industry makes on an area.

We're all aware of the holiday resorts which have been spoilt rotten by the onslaught of visitors. High-rise hotels sprawl across once beautiful landscapes, and it gets to the point where the original reason people visited a place – its beauty – has been totally destroyed.

Where you choose to holiday abroad says something about how you regard the treatment of other people living there. There are nations where the population lives under oppressive regimes, and which have a terrible history of human rights abuses. Amnesty International keeps comprehensive records of such countries and the Christian prisoners of conscience group Jubilee Campaign can inform you too.

It's fair enough to visit oppressive nations if you're there to work against the oppression. But to treat nations where people are tortured and killed for their beliefs and philosophies as holiday resorts strikes me as pretty insensitive. Then again, you could argue that most of the world is governed by some barbaric rules; even America has the death sentence, and we should take the log out of our own eyes.

When I was hostelling round Kenya — which itself has a dubious human rights record — I would occasionally bump into the same people. Some were 'doing' Africa, but I remember discussing with an Irish woman Alison, who was looking for teaching work in Kenya, how I couldn't understand why so many 'travellers' (to them, everyone else is a tourist) were heading for South Africa. Now maybe I'm naive, but I would suppose that people travelling through a continent would soon pick up the vibes of the way people are thinking. I felt that people travelling in a black person's continent would grow aware of their concern for blacks in South Africa. Now I accept that South Africa is supposed to be a stunning looking country, and worth seeing for that reason. But any white person used to our type of set-up in this country would surely feel very uncomfortable at the thought of the townships, of the 'whites-only' areas. And because they were white, unless they stuck their neck out they would have to go along with the white supremist opinions. But the travellers didn't seem to have any great qualms at all. Africa was there to be travelled through, it seemed, and political viewpoints and keeping your eyes open for what went on and not being racist were really inconveniences to the great adventure.

So it's important wherever we go for our hols — whether it's abroad, in another part of our country or close to home — to think about the local people and the impact of holiday-making on the local environment. Think about your destination, and keep your wits about you.

ACTION STATION

- Avoid buying souvenirs as much as possible. Instead take photos of the places you visit and have the most dramatic ones blown up into posters at Boots. Or collect natural objects to remind you of your travels, or do a daily sketch that will help you remember what you did and perhaps inspire you to be creative and make something of your holiday when you get back.

- Be prepared to stray off the beaten track when getting to know a place. Be careful not to damage the local habitat, and keep your eyes open so that you'll understand more of the area where you're holidaying.

- Talk to local people. Stay in the cheap B&Bs, guesthouses and lostels and you'll meet and chat to individuals and families who have their feet on the ground in the area.

- Have a go at *not* acting the tourist. If you're self-catering, don't bring the food with you, but buy it from local shops. Watch how the locals spend their days when they're not at work. Or get yourself a job to pay for your further travels and present upkeep and get right in there.

- Is there an out-of-bounds building you'd love to wander round or an organisation whose work you appreciate which you'd like to see at work? Write to the people or group who run it, explain your interest in the building – whether it's architectural or historical — and ask for a guided tour.

15

People in Greenhouses . . .

Christians certainly aren't the only people concerned about the environment, and at some point we have to decide whether or not we're going to get involved with Green groups that are not necessarily Christian.

Maybe this is not a problem for you. Like me, you were simply a Christian concerned about the environment and decided to join a group like Friends of the Earth so you could get active. Whether it was 'Christian' or not didn't really bother you.

But many believers find that they're not totally satisfied with what the non-Christian groups are saying, and so seek out other Christian Greens as a 'back-up'. Some people choose to be active purely with Christian organisations such as Christian Ecology Link or Animal Christian Concern. Others find that knowing that there are other Christians involved in the Green movement strengthens their own Green work, whatever organisation they happen to join.

Green Christians

I first wandered across the Christian Ecology Link (CEL) at the Greenbelt Festival when they were still known as the Christian Ecology Group. Currently the largest of the Christian Green organisations, it has established a network of local groups across the UK which aim to influence churches and bring a Christian perspective to local Green activities.

The Ripon Christian Ecology Group in Yorkshire is particularly active. It has sent bottles of Ecover washing-up liquid to local churches in an attempt to get them to use it, at least for the coffee cups. It arranges regular series of public talks on environmental topics, including a celebration of Rainforest Day with an illustrated lecture and discussion on local action. It also runs a programme of events that includes a nature walk with games for children and a 'flower trail' for adults, and involvement in a campaign to draw attention to the waste of paper, plastic and metal in unnecessary packaging of foodstuffs.

Ripon perhaps is a model example of a local Christian Green group. It ties in talks and discussions with a very attractive practical approach to Green living and is involved in the local church too. CEL produces *Root and Branch*[1] magazine for local groups where ideas for action are shared and Green Christians can find out about what's happening in their region – or start a group themselves.

At a national level the CEL tends to have a liberal Christian slant and evangelicals have not always been happy with the coverage given to New Age ideas in the quarterly newsletter *Green Christians*[2] and the Link's support of multi-faith services in the name of appreciation of the earth and its resources. And non-theologians and the mass of people in this country who haven't had access to higher education might be phased by its academic slant. Nevertheless, *Green Christians* is a useful starting point and provides plenty of information about other Green Christians that you can get in touch with. As I write, there is still sadly no evangelical equivalent.

Green giants
There is certainly a place for Christians to be active in Green but non-Christian organisations. As salt and light in God's world, there is potential for tremendous influence within the movement. Not in an over-the-top 'Here come the Christians' kind of way, but in a loving and gentle manner that beavers away getting things done for God.

Some Christians are very wary of the Green movement. They are worried at the apparent New Age hi-jack of Green concerns. Indeed, Tim Cooper, Joint National Co-ordinator of Christian Ecology Link, expressed concern that this attitude could deter Christians from getting involved in Green issues at all.

'They will avoid involvement in Green organisations through fear of being associated with the New Age. The crude analogy currently being made between the Green movement and New Age beliefs by some critics reveals a serious misunderstanding. Many evangelical Christians are already involved in Green organisations and to describe them as part of the New Age movement is quite wrong,' he warned.[3]

But the non-Christian Green organisations seem just as concerned at the New Age influence. I wrote to Friends of the Earth to complain about an advert they'd placed in the New Age 'bible', *Encyclopaedia Psychedelia*. It's a rather offensive full-colour glossy production featuring plenty of encouragement to try drugs, 'enlightenment' and clairvoyants, listing Sixties tune-in, drop-out guru Timothy Leary alongside Jesus Christ as someone worth following, and the edition I saw included an article describing Christ's crucified body in purely sexual terms.

I'd always respected Friends of the Earth since I got into Green thinking and I felt rather sad to see their advert in this unsavoury publication. But so did they.

'The tendency of the Green Movement to be linked to New Age philosophies is prevalent and as you point out, largely misleading and certainly not the direction we should be heading if we are to be recognised as the authoritative environmental movement we undoubtedly are,' FoE's Development Manager wrote back.[4] 'We do pride ourselves on the practical ways individuals can help save the environment at a local level,' she concluded.

And so they should. FoE is probably the best organisation to join if you want to change things Greenly in your local community. Its head office is involved in national and international research and campaigns while it retains a grass roots activism around the country. Young people are also catered for through its daughter body Earth Action aimed at people aged from fourteen to twenty-three years, with a very inspiring magazine *EAR* (Earth Action Report).[5] A series of Days of Action are aimed at publicising and raising awareness on particular environmental issues. It seems a long way away from my days as a sixth form Greenie when I was the youngest regular attender by about twenty years at the local Hilingdon FoE meetings.

As one of the larger environmental organisations Greenpeace has done some extremely valuable work in publicising the destruction of the planet via its very upfront, confrontational approach. Yet if you personally are itching to get active, then Greenpeace is unlikely to fulfil that need. Its work relies on a small core team of experts, researchers and activists, and the rest of us are encouraged to collect money to help support their action. They're well worth supporting, but it's also wise to find out what you can do Greenly at a community level.

Life and soul of the party
Some committed Greens refer to the Big Three organisations as Friends of the Earth, Greenpeace, and the Green Party. They all have their role to play in raising Green awareness and trying to change things.

But when it comes to party politics, Christians shouldn't automatically sign up with the Greens if they're environmentally conscious. God wants some of His people on the Government side, and some backing the Opposition too in order to get His work done. No one party is *the* one Christians should vote for. So it's up to us to consider our political views in a Christian light, and pray about our involvement with a particular group, whether that's giving them a cross on a ballot paper or

becoming fully active at a national level. Whatever
political party we decide to support, we bring a valuable
Christian and Green perspective to their work.

It's worth considering whether or not you're going to
contribute anything to the specifically Christian versions
of the political spectrum. As well as the cross-party
Christian Ecology Link, there are bodies representing
Christian Socialists, Democrats, Social Democrats,
Conservatives and Liberal Democrats, so you should be
able to find something that suits you!

Animal passions

'Contemporary commercial and social exploitation of
animals has gone beyond the bounds of any com-
passionate Christian understanding. I think of intensive
farming, vivisection, bloodsports, luxury fur . . .' states
May Tripp of Animal Christian Concern,[1] a worthy
evangelical organisation sounding a clear Christian voice
in a field where activists are notoriously anti-Christian
because of our complacency towards animals.

The ACC has organised specifically Christian services
– as opposed to multi-faith ones – to pray for animals,
for our forgiveness for the way we treat them, and for
an end to cruel and exploitative practices.

It's worth backing up our prayers for animals and our
concern for animals with information supplied by such
groups as Compassion in World Farming, Animal Aid,
The Vegetarian Society and the Royal Society for the
Protection of Birds. All have their youth groups.

Going, going green

And you can bring your specifically Christian and Green
values to groups that on the surface appear quite
unconnected with environmental issues. Indeed, both the
Scouts and the Guides have adopted Green practices as
a result of the growing Green concern among the
population and its members.

Whatever organisations you're involved with, think about ways that you can introduce your views to the others members and the powers that be. You should discover that at least some of the others are very keen to be Green and value the presence of another Green sympathiser. Join with them to strengthen your call.

We shouldn't be afraid of other organisations and their Green activism. Rather, celebrate the fact that it's not just a number of Christians that are concerned about the planet we live on. It's up to us to work alongside them, showing God's way, whether that's in a specifically Christian group or in the same organisation.

ACTION STATION

- Send for a copy of *Liberation of Life*, the world Council of Churches' report on the Christian attitude to human, animal and environmental matters. Price 65p from Inter-Church House, 35–41 Lower Marsh, London SE1 7RL.

- Look for details in your local paper about Green groups close to home. Go along to some of their meetings to find out which suits you the best, and get active there.

- Have a Green money box into which you can put spare change and give the money to bodies which need funds for research and other headquarters responsibilities.

16

The Sky's the Limit

Our degradation of the environment doesn't just affect the world we live on. It touches the atmosphere around the earth too. Chemicals in the smoke from industrial chimneys and car exhausts float over nations and fall as acid rain. The ozone hole widens over both the Poles and lets in the sun's harmful rays that scorch our bodies and the land. Pollutants rise into the atmosphere and collect where, like the glass of a Greenhouse, they as a barrier keeping the heat in and the temperature of the planet creeps upwards.

The technicolour satellite images of an ozone hole the size of the USA over Antarctica really made people sit up and take notice. Here was the ghastly evidence that we'd gone too far. CFC in aerosols, moulded fast food cartons and fridges began to be phased out. There was no option — we had to change our lifestyles in some way. To address the *big* environmental issues that touch the sky, avoid using aerosols and reduce your use of electricity and travelling by car.

Sky writing
But we can see hope too — in the beauty of the sky and the message of new beginnings it brings each day. God has control over the heavens and the earth. The winds and waves obey Him.[1]

Through the stunning image of the rainbow He makes a covenant, an agreement with us: 'I have set my rainbow in the clouds, and it will be the sign of the covenant for all generations to come . . . it will be the sign of the covenant between me and the earth. Whenever I bring clouds over the earth and the rainbow appears in the clouds, I will remember my covenant between me and you and all living creatures of every kind. Never again will the waters become a flood to destroy all life.'[2]

It's not just the rainbow that sends out messages. It's not by accident that we say 'red sky at night, shepherd's delight, red sky in the morning, shepherd's warning'. It's a truth that's been absorbed into folklore over the centuries. And out of our 'natural' 1990s habitat, it's amazing how quickly we resort to relying on God's signs of nature to direct us.

I *should* know, but I'm afraid I've never fathomed out how to find north using a watch and the sun. If the light's too bright, you can't see the digital numbers . . . But we do have a natural body clock; just to be awkward it runs on a twenty-five hour cycle, but nevertheless it works very well if you line it up with the sun's position in the sky.

My friend Juliet and I once spent a week youth hostelling around the Lake District. For some unknown reason, neither of us had a watch. We would set off from one hostel each morning to arrive at a different one in the evening. During the day, we'd rarely see a soul and spent most of the time walking in the hills. But within a few days we were both amazed at how accurate my timekeeping had become. By taking note of the time when we left the hostel or if we happened to pass through a village – which wasn't frequent – and checking how high the sun was in the sky, and with a bit of what turned out to be fairly reliable guesswork on how many hours we'd been walking, it became quite possible to tell the time. And we'd stroll down the valley to the next hostel, confident that we were early enough to grab a couple of the bottom bunks.

Of course, out in the middle of nowhere you don't actually need to be too accurate, but it's helpful just to know the time roughly, and we do adjust incredibly quickly. But back in the city, it's practically impossible to tell the time from the sky, just because there are too many clocks and it's easier to ask.

These days, I rely on my well-spoken mate TIM, the speaking clock. It's about time I got a watch. But when I do get round to getting one I'll make sure it's a good traditional wind-up that if taken care of should last a lifetime, rather than a digital which would need to be kept fed with batteries. You might consider doing the same.

Sun strokes

No wonder people once worshipped the sun. After a cold, damp and grey British winter, people ache for a bit of brightness. Indeed some people do go slow during the dark months as if their bodies are telling them that it's time to hibernate, and the UK suicide rate tends to be highest in January and February.

My father, who lived in India well into his twenties, recalls how during his first British winter in the Fifties, he couldn't work out what the strange muted round orange glow in the sky was. When it clicked that it was actually the sun, he tells me his heart sank. Used to the vibrant light and heat of an Indian sun, he must have felt very cold and swallowed up by the grey, foggy air.

These days we no longer have those thick curling fogs, and the sun seems to have got hotter. Indeed the temperatures of the summers of the 1980s were abnormally high. Maybe they were first signs of the Greenhouse Effect – the warming of the atmosphere under a cloud of pollution – or maybe it was just a perfectly normal abnormality.

Some people are determined to look on the bright side. If those hot summers were a taste of summers to come, then they admit to looking froward to the full-blown Greenhouse Effect. After all, Britons will enjoy a Mediterranean climate without having to go overseas, they smile . . .

Sure, Christians should be hopeful, but we shouldn't

be short-sighted or inconsiderate about what's going on in the rest of the world. Lots of sunshine might make us Brits more open, fun-loving and relaxed, but we need to think how it will affect other parts of the planet. Vast tracts of Africa and the Continent will be uninhabitable. People *and* animals will have to migrate to survive, crops will shrivel, rivers dry up, and we'll have to protect our eyes and our skin from the heat of the sun. No doubt tans will go out of fashion. And I haven't even mentioned the melting of the ice-caps and the flooding of the world's low-lying areas including Britain's coastline and river-based cities.

Personally, I've found the recent UK summers *too* hot. Rolling up your sleeves to catch a tan is one thing, but the sun's rays have proved uncomfortably scorching. And that worries me. On those golden summer days I'm afraid I find it difficult to thank God for the 'good' weather we've been having. Part of me is worried that our human greed, our overuse of resources, has got the upper-hand. Perhaps we shouldn't be thanking God for the sunshine, but asking Him to forgive us for our arrogance and selfishness that have affected the world's weather.

Night moves

If the sun is too high in the sky for our liking, we can always wait until dark. What goes on then can be just as interesting as what happens in daylight and shows us something of God's glow of pure light through the night of life on earth. On a sweltering evening it's very peaceful to go for a walk in the dark with friends. Or sit in your back garden or the local park and chat and watch the sun go down.

If you live in an area such as the Fens where the land is flat, you get some tremendous panoramic views of the sky. After a month in Norway where the evening skies are out of this world (well, they would be . . .), I spent a year in Cambridge. My eyes more open to the delights

147

of just looking at the sky and appreciating God's handiwork, I witnessed some stunning sights.

One evening strolling back to my college which was a bit out of the town centre, I happened to turn to look back at the ancient buildings. I was awestruck at the blood-red sky that sat heavily around them. The rich crimson spread over the night sky, and I just stood, my head tilted full back, enjoying the view with amazement and pleasure.

If you're a townie, you'll have to journey away to experience the true darkness of the night. There are just too many lights in urban areas for you to get a clear picture. Indeed, satellite pictures of the UK at night show few areas untouched by the glow of cities.

Out in the countryside you can be surrounded by black. On a clear night the constellations of the stars are very sharp and it's fun to name the ones you can see. As the names were given to them so long ago, why not try and think up new ones after images that they seem to represent. Certainly you can recognise an old-style plough, but to my eye the Plough looks more like a saucepan. Make up new constellations from the array of stars you can see. After all, though the Plough groups together seven very bright stars, most of them seem to be just random collections of a few close stars combined with the strong imagination of the Ancient Greeks.

The Plough is quite distinct, and if you're in unfamiliar territory, it can be quite heartwarming to see a familiar sight. But does the group of stars that makes up Orion really look like a figure of a man? Why did they choose those particular stars to group together and not others? Though the place of each star has been marked out by God, on a clear night when the stars seem particularly bright, the night sky can seem like a massive join-the-dots without any numbers.

Just looking heavenwards at the sky calms us down. It's a very restful activity that takes us out of ourselves.

It can make us feel very small and insignificant, so no wonder people like to think that there's life on other planets out there. As Christians we should be struck by God's amazing creation that reaches out so far beyond our own world.

On my travels in Kenya, I ended up in Lamu, a very pleasant Muslim village full of cats and donkeys, narrow streets and cafés overflowing with delicious yogurt drinks. And rambling flat-roofed buildings where you could sleep up top during the hot nights. It's an experience to lie under the blanket of a black sky sprinkled with shooting stars, and be woken at 5am the next morning by the echoing prayers of the Muslims.

Darkness can draw us closer to God. Whether you're out in the open air or in your bedroom with the light turned off, the blackness helps us to block out distractions. In some ways I imagine it's a bit like floating in one of those desensitiser tanks. Being in complete darkness, all you can see is black. You can feel totally alone except for the presence of God. It's you and He together in the quiet. Thank God for the different times of day that enable you to pray in different kinds of ways.

Whatever the weather
What of the droughts and floods that destroy life regularly somewhere in the world? And the storms that rage?

In this country we're fairly well protected. Our homes are fairly solid, and if they are damaged, we might be re-housed, or insurance can pay for the destruction. In other lands, a whole village might be destroyed and people left without any belongings. Gloria, a Jamaican friend, tells me that 'in Jamaica you don't get any of this fancy rain that you have here. It suddenly comes straight down and just as suddenly stops. So if people have been building a road, then it's washed away. If they've been erecting phone and power lines, they've been torn down.'

Look at the map of Bangladesh and you'll see that the country is basically a river's flood plain, and that the water doesn't have to rise that much for homes and farmland to be washed away. Tear Fund working with partners HEED Bangladesh has helped build 'khillas' — large mounds of earth — on which people now live with their animals and grow crops, safe from the almost annual floodings. Write to Tear Fund for further information about the project, and organise fund-raising events (Tear Fund has a list of 100 ideas for these as well) to support the khilla programme.

Protecting the sky is a daunting task. Climate too seems well beyond our reach when it comes to wanting better weather, and protecting the environment, people and animals. But there are small and positive moves we can make.

And we can respond to the damage weather causes by supporting the work of organisations like Tear Fund which are actively helping people who suffer from bad weather. God is working through them to control the wind and the rain.

ACTION STATION

- At the top of a hill or in a very flat treeless region, look upwards at the sky and take in the view. Offer the moment to God.

- Whenever you have a bonfire, avoid burning plastics, which give off poisonous fumes into the air.

- Avoid using aerosols. Ask yourself if you need the product anyway, whatever container it's in.

17

Hands Across the Ocean

The environmental crisis of the hole in the ozone layer and the Greenhouse Effect has make it quite clear that wherever we live on this planet we're all at threat. But if we're going to worry about the problem and do something in response, our action shouldn't just be aimed at the Western world. We have to think about our brothers and sisters on the other side of the world too.

The way we live here affects how people live elsewhere. As the main culprits of the destruction of the environment because of our materialistic and industry-based lifestyles, it is our responsibility to ensure that other people will no longer suffer through our greed.

We must make it our business to learn about how the Western world depends on the developing nations, and keeps poor countries poor and people starving by buying goods at rock-bottom prices. Read New Internationalist magazine[1] and write to the World Development Movement and Christian Aid for information about world trade.

Mahatma Gandhi said, 'There is enough for every man's need, but not every man's greed.' He was revealing that if we only bothered to share world resources more equally, everybody would be happy. We in the West live well beyond the world's means. Sure, in the planet's present state we can have a comfortable life, but it's only at the expense of smaller and poorer nations. Ours is not a just lifestyle.

And the world couldn't stand it if the Third World suddenly gained equality with its wealthy Western neighbours. If all the people in the world lived as you and I do, there wouldn't be much of the world left. That's not an excuse to switch off now and continue living like we do, but a reason why we should reduce our standard of living and consume more carefully. If only we were willing to make some sacrifices and trade on a fair basis with other countries instead of resorting to greed, then Third World countries would have some chance of breaking out of the poverty chain that imprisons them.

Mythbreaking

There are a lot of untruths and assumptions about the reasons people in the Third World live in poverty. By checking the facts, we soon realise how similar are we humans across the world. We laugh, weep, hurt, grieve, relax, work, have fun in basically similar ways, yet our circumstances are very different.

From a Christian perspective, we can literally say 'There but for the grace of God go I', yet work from that standpoint and try and do something to support people so that they can climb out of their poverty. We can give them, as one charity slogan once declared, 'a hand up, not a hand out'. If we care about the world's people, then it's up to us to stand with them when others criticise or are just ignorant of why people live a particular way. Let's look at some of the things people say.

• *'They have too many children . . .'*
The death rate is high in the Third World so having large families gives hope that at least one of the children will reach adulthood, and later on look after their parents in their old age.

Having a big family is not what pulls a family into poverty, but instead a clinging onto life with the hope that survivors of the next generation will rise out of the poverty cycle.

If you ever get to see a family tree of your ancestors in the last century, you'll see a similar pattern. Many

153

children died before they reached their fifth birthday. There may have been some of the trappings of an industrialised nation – many family trees are listed in weighty family Bibles – but their situation was otherwise very similar to may who live in developing countries today.

And don't believe it when anybody tells you that Third World mothers are so used to losing their babies that another death in the family doesn't really matter that much. Women in developing countries are like women anywhere. 'Can a woman forget her own baby and not love the child she bore?'[2] These suffering people believe in a future for their children. They hope their girls and boys will outlive them. And like any mother, they simply love their children. To see child after child fade away and die must tear their hearts apart.

- *'They're just not capable of getting themselves organised.'*

The human race is community based, and in rural societies in particular there is a close-knit network of people with a role to suit the needs and abilities of each person.

But because Third World countries developed quickly under Western rule, they've never been given the chance to evolve naturally. Many of the patterns of farming and society are culturally unnatural. Developing countries are littered with Western equipment that wasn't suited to the environment or economy. In Africa, the boundaries of countries actually cut across tribal territories, cutting communities in half and forcing people into relationships with traditional enemies. When states have become independent, it's no wonder that civil unrest is common.

And as many of the countries' leaders, though native to the country, have been educated in the elitist public schools and universities of the West, it's questionable how relevant their education is to the actual needs of their countries' ordinary and less privileged people.

But that's not to say that ordinary people in developing countries aren't doing their bit to turn the tide of environmental destruction. In Kenya, for example, the Green Belt Movement − a tree-planting initiative by women's groups across the nation − has proved to be a resounding success at a grass roots level.

- *'Poor soil and poor climate mean they're fighting a losing battle against poverty.'*

Certainly the rains do fail, and the deserts are spreading at an alarming rate, but these are as much the symptoms of the Third World's poverty as the cause. Many of the developing countries are potentially some of the most fertile in the world. Just consider where the exotic fruit and veg you can buy at your local greengrocer have come from.

Much of the good soil has in fact been bought up by large multi- or trans-national companies to supply *us* with food, leaving the locals with the remains of the land. The poorer soil is less fertile and so communities must search further and further afield for land where they can grow their own supplies. Trees are cut down for firewood and building materials and so that the land beneath can be used. Soil is eventually blown away and the land turns to desert. Without the trees and plants, it's harder for warm air to rise and form rain clouds to wash the earth.

By supporting organisations like Traidcraft, you're helping people take control of their own environment by growing and selling produce to the developed world − and ploughing the proceeds back into the local communities. It's about giving people space so they've enough land on which to survive with some left over so that the land can thrive and the weather improve.

- *'People in the Third World are just too lazy to get themselves out of poverty.'*

If you think you've got it tough studying at school or working shifts or a nine-to-five job, spare a thought for

155

families in the developing world where children are helping with the family workload as soon as they can walk.

If they choose not to work — or simply are not well enough — there's no social security or National Health Service to fall back on. The vast majority of people simply cannot survive without having to work hard, whether paid or unpaid. Women trek miles every day to collect buckets of water which they carry on their heads back to their homes. Children as young as five beg, shoeshine or sell papers, sweets and their services to keep their families afloat.

Unless you're rich in the Third World, and few are, you don't have much choice about what work to do. You simply get on and do what needs to be done. Laziness is a luxury.

- *'They're practically living in the Stone Age; just look at the primitive tools they use for farming. No wonder they have problems.'*

People in the developing world use what we in the industrialised West would class as primitive implements, simply because in their present situation they are the best tools for the job. It's no use using tractors and combine harvesters if you haven't access to oil or money to pay for it when the vehicles need a top up, or the spare parts when they break down.

The wooden and metal tools have proved themselves through the centuries. In many places instruments and farming methods have changed little since Bible times. They reveal humanity's resourcefulness with the essentials God's put on the earth. Certainly the West can bring mechanical expertise and new ideas to the Third World, but we have much to learn too from the poorer countries' initiative, use of basics, simplicity and survival instincts that we've lost since the Industrial Revolution.

- *'There's no hope for the Third World. They can only
  survive with our handouts; otherwise they'd starve.'*
It's easy to get the impression that the people of the
developing world are totally dependent on us. The images
we get from the media don't always help. Indeed, a survey
at a London school revealed that the schoolchildren's
general impression was that Ethiopians were always
starving, covered in flies, pot bellied, queuing for food,
being weighed or injected by white doctors and
nurses . . .

Successful projects and old-fashioned living don't get
a look-in. Let's face it, images of happy, reasonably
healthy communities going about their day-to-day
business don't make good TV! So when droughts and
famines end and people start getting back to normality,
the film teams and reporters tend to wander away.

And if you think that the Geldof extravaganza and the
giving it all motivated was a mammoth effort — and it
was — pause to consider that for every £1 given by this
country in aid to the Third World during Live Aid year,
£9 was clawed back by our Government through trade
tariffs and debt repayment. Who's dependent on whom?

Helping hand

Like other charities and agencies, Christian bodies
working in the Third World have come to realise that a
concern for the condition of the environment must go
hand-in-hand with development programmes if countries
are to step out of poverty and remain out.

In Zaire, the Salvation Army has a travelling rural
development project that trains local people in tree
planting and bee keeping. World Vision not only helped
tell the world about the 1984 Ethiopian famine by flying
in the news team that first recorded it for TV, but also
assembled 'Agpaks' of agricultural supplies including
farm tools, seeds, three months' worth of rations to last
until harvest, and oxen for ploughing and livestock for

new herds for the stricken Ansokia region to help the farmers get back on their feet. They supported local people in restoring the desert valley − used as a feeding centre during the famine − to make it resistant to future drought and famine through a water programme, erosion control projects, and a reforestation campaign which involved the planting of millions of trees.

'The valley of Ansokia, now green from end to end, feeding itself and exporting food, is only one of many cases of self-sustaining development created in Ethiopia since the mid-1980s. Together they offer both hope and proof that the nation can rise to self-sufficiency,' reveals Bruce Brander, reporting for World Vision.[3]

Being there
There are many Christian mission and relief organisations with partners in developing countries where you can be of service. For most, you must be aged eighteen or over and it helps if you've a useful practical skill, though for many enthusiasm for service is just as important.

Many short-term projects take place during the summer months, so are ideal as part of a year out or 'holiday' between study. They should open your eyes too and extend your understanding of the world beyond the UK. And if you're too young to get stuck in at the moment, it's worth sending off for information now just so that you're aware of the possibilities and of any skills or interests that are needed, and so are more ready for action when the time comes.

Once you've been working full-time for a few years you could well be eligible for a number of years of VSO work − Voluntary Service Overseas. It's a way of putting to use the skills you've obtained over here, over there.

ACTION STATION

- Read:
  A World of Difference by Simon Jenkins (Lion Educational, 1988).
  Who Profits? by Richard Adams (Lion).

- Send for Tear Fund's *Fundraising: 101 Ways To Help* leaflet. Send an A4 sized SAE to Tear Fund, 100 Church Road, Teddington, Middlesex TW11 8QE.

- Contact one of the Third World organisation at the end of this book to be put on their mailing list for information. Consider hiring a film or video and invite freinds round to your church hall or your home to watch and discuss the issues raised.

- Visit your library or museum and find out about crafts and products made in the Third World. Have a go at crafts like spinning and weaving, hand-dyeing and carpentry.

- Show others how the other Two-Thirds live. Build a shanty hut and get people to sponsor you to stay in it. And explain to them how a lot of the people in the world — including people in this country — must live day-to-day in such shacks.

18

Whose World
Is It Anyway?

However active we are in looking after God's world, we must never forget that it is His. God created the universe and delights in His creation. The plants and creatures which flourish across the world are there for His pleasure.

It is something to bear in mind when the world's environmental problems seem too big for us to make a difference. We *can* feel washed out by our activities and though we give the burden to Christ, we may still worry about how little we seem to be doing. But *whatever* we do do Green-wise in His name, we do it for Him.

After a rain shower when you're walking along the street and spot a worm in the middle of the pavement, it's an act of Christian charity to pick it up − use a twig if like me you're squeamish − and put it on a patch of grass or mud so it doesn't dry out on the concrete but can burrow away. Scientist friends may tell you that worms aren't conscious creatures, that they're just a bunch of coldblooded cells that wriggle around. But worms are still God's and therefore part of His great plan. Likewise, don't squash insects and spiders that enter your house, but use a lidded dustpan or a glass and a piece of card to take them outside.

Such actions, and indeed such creatures might seem insignificant in the Great Scheme of Things. But they weren't too insignificant for God to bother about, and so if we find them crossing our path, then why not take care rather than crush them under our feet as if they're not worth anything.

In control

Can we command these little creatures in God's name to sit still while we take them to a safer place? If we're troubled by wild animals or irritating insects can we ask them 'in the name of Jesus' to leave us alone? Certainly there is a Christian tradition of living side-by-side with animals. Indeed everyone living in a rural community must share their land with wild creatures. It is said that in the fourth century St Anthony found that animals looking for water had invaded his Egyptian garden. He gently took one aside and told it to 'Go away and in the Lord's name do not come near these things again.' And they went.[1]

Is this so strange? We pray for God to protect us, and if we happened to be faced with a wild beast, God would take command over the situation and choose whether we escaped untouched. And if I were in the grip of a Rottweiler's jaws, desperate prayer would certainly be one of my ways of fighting back.

I have a strange fear of those large black house spiders, the type that tend to stay put in the corners of the ceiling or just as likely dash across the carpet as you're watching TV. I can handle other crawlies and don't mind them fluttering or taking a walk within my cupped hands as I take them into the garden. And funnily enough, I have no real problems with covering a house spider with a glass, slipping a postcard underneath, flipping the thing over and taking it outside – as long as the card doesn't move.

But if one of those things crawled over me I would, to put it rather melodramatically, 'just die'. Basically, and rather irrationally, I know, the thought of one touching me terrifies me.

I can trace my fear right back to a childhood trauma. These days, you're encouraged to face your phobia. But I can face it – sharing the same room, it being in a container that's moved closer and closer to me. I can

161

handle that, and can just about face the point when they take the lid off. It's when the therapist holds it and expects to pass it to my hands that I would flee. I don't want to hold a house spider. It's like my friend Brenda who's afraid of flying. Understandably she has no desire to go up in a plane to overcome it.

And I just happen to live in this old rambling and rotting vicarage that is probably – and I'm not going to start looking for them – crawling with these things. I woke up one night to the sound of one of them scrabbling over the papers I'd left on the floor. I turned on the light to see it shoot across the carpet.

So what can I do? The only thing I can do is pray. I pray that God won't test me, because I just don't feel up to it – though of course He doesn't put us in situations that He won't help us handle. And I pray that if one of those spiders must crawl over me while I'm in bed – and that's where I feel most vulnerable – that's fine by me, as long as I'm completely oblivious to it. I want to be out cold when it happens. And God has honoured that.

God tames the savage animal as He pleases. He is Lord over all the world and though much of it is controlled by Satan, it is still God's. The creatures of the earth will be still as He asks, the winds and waves obey Him.

'Despite the obvious presence of evil, God is still sovereign and the world is still God's world. As He has worked to create it, so we, as one of His trustees for our own lifespan, must work to look after His masterpiece. There is no great gulf between religious and material, between spirit and matter. God Himself created matter, He organised it by orderly laws in one rational, uniform stable system . . .'[2]

Simply valued
Very popular among conservationists, whether Christian or not, are the creatures and plants of the tropical rainforests. Yet it's interesting to see that the arguments put forward in favour of saving the world's rainforests are often based on the potential *use* of what lives there.

A lot of modern medicine has been developed from plants so, people suggest, a cure for a deadly illness such as AIDS may well be lurking in the forests. If the trees are cut down, they argue, humanity will have lost an answer to one of its grave problems.

But no loud voice has pointed out that we should protect the forests for their own sake, that their inhabitants are valuable simply because they exist, and that the world loses out from their potential non-existence.

God delights in His creation and it must sadden Him to see how we plunder its riches and treat it with so much disrespect, and lock its stunning creatures into cages where many of them lose their minds, while we flatten their habitat so that they can never return to the wild.

The best treatment?
It's our job while we're here to help Him put it right and work towards a better way of treating His planet. Though

we can feel disheartened too. There's something about animals that touches us. I hope that it's not just the Walt Disney factor that gives them cuddly characteristics they don't actually have. Nature *is* red in tooth and claw. And certainly there are poisonous plants and creatures like the great white shark, alligators, plagues of locusts and a range of dangerous snakes that we should be careful of. Nevertheless the natural world has an enormous vulnerability and a lot to fear from us.

I recall meeting an ordinary bloke a few years ago in a fish and chip shop in the Kew Road after I'd been to a Richmond and Twickenham Green Party meeting. I was wearing a Green badge and we got talking about the destruction of the environment, and he told me of a documentary he'd seen on the rainforests. There'd been a shot of a sloth calmly hanging from a branch just doing its thing, while metres below a chain saw chewed away at the base of the tree. And the guy told me how that scene had really hit him.

William Kolzwinkle's novel *Doctor Rat*[3] is notable for its vivid descriptions of how humanity plays havoc with the animal world. Yes, it includes a tale of a sloth losing its grip, but the most moving piece for me was the image of a golden eagle trapped inside a cage, and its thoughts of open skies.

Creature comfort

As Christians whatever we do to God's creatures on earth − and we do some grim things in the name of scientific research, farming, sport and controlling populations — we have hope that these animals will be renewed in Heaven. The lion will lie down with the lamb.

It'll be good to see happy animals in Heaven, and ones that have long since vanished from the earth — the dodo, and all those marvellous creatures whose fossils and bones are on show at London's Natural History Museum. Imagine praising God from the back of a tyrannosaurus rex! Of course, this is all imagining, but why not? As Cliff Richard says, think of the most amazing tropical beach you've seen − whether on the box or if you've been fortunate enough to visit. Well, in heaven it'll be better than that!

Of course, none of us really knows what Heaven's going to be like, but the Bible gives us a few clues about the harmony and perfection of Creation praising Jesus for ever. And so some of the most surreal images, like the dinosaur giving rides, can't help springing to mind. And even then our imaginations are incomplete and just can't really fathom what God has in store.

Artists of any field help us see other ways of sensing the world. Christian artists are motivated and inspired by God, and though our sinful nature clouds the truth in the artist's work and our interpretation of it, He does speak through it.

Just the idea of God moulding the potter at his wheel shaping clay is one to dwell on. Chris Eaton who wrote the beautiful song 'Discovering' (on Cliff's *Now You See Me, Now You Don't* album[4]) has said that he really felt God guiding what he wrote. And you can tell because it talks right through to your soul.

Prayer, when it's in the hands of the Holy Spirit, takes our feeble words and changes them into sheer poetry. Not every Christian 'speaks in tongues' whether this is interpreted as being good at earthly languages or communicating with God in heavenly words. Yet God uses whatever language limitations we might have, and fashions words of truth out of the words we can use. We don't have to be great intellects or highly articulate. Indeed some people are so wordy that they intellectualise God out of existence by their huge vocabulary, while the prayers of the not-so-bright and of children hold deep truths despite their basic language. Out of the mouths of babes come touching words of great beauty. It is the art of voice.

Art in the right hands shows us the world through God's eyes. When we mix paints from the palette of our own experiences, from what we see in pictures and the environment around us, we can't help but get the impression that He must have had a marvellous time creating the universe. God let His imagination run riot.

ACTION STATION

- Look for God in the world around you. Ask Him to show you the world as He sees it. Get a sketch book and scribble down some of the things you see. Or use a cheap camera and snap the scenes that remind you of Him.

- If you have a pet, watch it. Take responsibility for its upkeep. Befriend it in God's name.

- Maybe you've generally found nature programmes on the box a bit of a drag. Make the effort to watch and listen the next time a wildlife programme is scheduled. Look at the landscapes, the creatures' habitats and the way they live. Open your eyes to the wonders of this world.

- If ever you're wandering round churches, check to see how God's world is portrayed in stained glass windows, stonework and banners. Often they tell of our inter-relationship with the rest of the world. Stop awhile and ponder and pray about the scenes you see.

- If you have a place in the world that God has moved you to pray for, find out as much as you can about that place. Learn about the people

---

and pray for them, but think also about the environment in which they live, and the creatures they share it with.

- Visit art exhibitions to see the different ways that people view the world. While you're looking at different artwork ask God to show you what reflects His truth. Read about different art techniques to understand the reasoning behind different styles. See the world from different angles and lit by God.

19

The Offering

As Christians we have given ourselves to God. Our Green concern flows from Him and in the way we choose to live we offer it back to Him. But we can give more by using the money we earn or receive in pocket-money, pay or clothes allowance to extend His Kingdom.

Time to tithe

Many Christians give a tenth of their income to the work of the Church. It's a helpful way of making sure that at least some of our finances go to God.

It's better to know that at least part of our money is going to God and has been allocated to go to Him, rather than just thinking about giving some money away, but not really being sure how much and never getting round to doing it. With tithing it's easy to work out how much of your income to give away — just move the decimal point one place to the left. And if you separate it out as soon as you get your money you'll soon find that you automatically think of the remaining figure as the money that'll pay for all your other needs.

But we must be careful what we do with this remaining money we have. We must remember that although it is not part of our tithe, it still belongs to God. If one penny in every ten pence we are given goes to, say, help the people of the Third World, then we must be very careful that the remaining nine aren't spent on goods or activities that not only satisfy our selfishness, but exploit the world's land and people at the same time.

It's no good, for example, giving money to Tear Fund, Traidcraft or Christian Aid if we buy food produced by a company that knowingly exploits the people and land of Third World countries. If we don't even think about what we do with the remaining 90 per cent of our money and are supporting unjust trading operations, then our tithe becomes worthless through our own lack of care.

But who to give it to? There are so many charities and good causes vying for our attention that it can be difficult to decide what to do with our money. Some people, particularly church treasurers, would rather you gave your tithe to the local church. If you don't earn much or only get pocket-money, this might be the best place for you to put a weekly sum.

Maybe you don't want to see your money end up paying for the church roof – which is understandable. But it can be argued that if every Christian gave their thithe to their church, the nation's Church would be much more effective, and it could afford to take on board more important causes at a local, national and international level. And this would show the strength and unity of the Church. 'The more the giving is associated with the church collectively, the more it is attributed to the Christian faith and the less to our individual merit.'[1]

Outside of church life, it's really up to you and God what you do with your tithe. He will show you where the need is and our reasons for giving. 'The causes and the people to whom we give should be on our prayer list. If they are worth giving to, they are worth praying for. If we pray thoughtfully and intelligently, we can hardly fail to give with more thought and intelligence. As we pray for a cause, we realise that we could help with money too.'[2]

Some people don't believe in giving to charity as they feel the Government should be helping the needy. Others have favourite issues, say, homelessness, that they want to support. Some will only back projects that focus on moral issues. Others will prefer to concentrate on one-offs, using their money to help people in need when they come across them. Through prayer, God shows us where our priorities should lie.

Because you're drawn to environmental issues, you'll want to support projects that help the earth fight back. Maybe you're particularly concerned about animals so you'll want to give to animal groups. Incidentally, a number of them including the RSPCA and the British Union for the Abolition of Vivisection were started by Christians in the last century as part of the great movement of Christian social action. There are organisations and charities dealing with most Green issues, so you should be able to find one to suit your interests.

Most of the bodies that work in the environmental field are non-Christian, so be sure to balance out your giving to them by giving to Christian groups too. Not that God doesn't work through unbelievers; just look what He did with Band Aid. But Christian organisations have the added dimension of faith in Jesus which motivates their work, and should be giving the glory back to Him.

The middle man

Money, if we're not careful, can act very much like the proverbial 'middle man'. It can distance us from people both near and far, getting between real relationships. Money buys isolation. Instead of being prepared to share and swap the talents and possessions we have, we put a price on what we own and become entwined in the money system. For the flipside to suggesting that it's only when you have money that you can help others, is to suggest that without money you can't do anything. And neither Christianity nor Green thinking believes that.

Certainly it helped that the Good Samaritan had money to pay the innkeeper to look after the injured man. But the point about the parable is that the Good Samaritan cared.[3] There are plenty of unsung heroes across the world who just have to get on with caring, feeding the hungry, healing the sick whether or not they've got the cash. And money when it does matter doesn't go into huge glamorous schemes but low-key community projects using local people and local materials that help the people help themselves.

We get into the bad habit of thinking that we should be involved in the big expensive projects, when God is happy with us working for Him on our doorsteps, being good neighbours, visiting the sick and housebound, looking out for the lonely, being able to put an arm around somebody who has just been bereaved, getting local people working together and helping each other. And financially that doesn't cost anything.

And the whole Green ethos of Acting Local and Thinking Globally works very well at this level. Actions do have a knock-on effect. If a team of you in your street organise a Green scheme, such as a collection of materials that can be recycled, everybody soon gets the message that resources are valuable, and that just because they don't personally have a use for something doesn't mean that somebody else won't.

As children we would take the accumulated family collection of milk bottle tops and aluminium foil across the road to elderly Mrs Steer who'd give us a toffee in return. She gave the foil to the Guide Dogs for the Blind. In Germany at fixed times in the year, maybe once a month, people put their unwanted furniture and possessions into the street so that others can have a rummage and take what they want.

When it comes to doing God's work, it doesn't matter if you don't have much money. He knows our circumstances. He wants us to do as much as we can with the resources He has given us; Jesus explains this in the parable of the talents.[4] In fact, we can sometimes be more effective, both as Christians and as Greens, when we put finances to the back of our minds and just get stuck in.

Can't buy me love

Money gets between people. It puts a false value on people and possessions. In his book *Who Switched the Price Tags?* Tony Campolo suggests that it's as if somebody came along in the night and put high price tags on all the valueless things, and low price tags on the things that really matter.[5] Just compare, for example, how much teachers, nurses and others who work in caring and serving professions get paid with the amount earned by people in the less sacrificial jobs such as advertising, pop music, stockbroking and TV presenting.

God's way turns the world's values on their head. He values and loves each one of us because we are His. We look at the world and see His creation and its value because he created it. Once His, He gives us a heart for His world, and with it a new way of living. We learn the importance of relationships, of caring, of giving ourselves – of love in the situations we find ourselves in. And though that *is* costly in terms of time, patience and friendship, it doesn't need to cost a penny.

Walking with Christ is about choosing His way at each step. And God's ways are both very simple and very deep.

Certainly, we can use money to express our horror or sadness at suffering and pay to help stop it at the same time. I recall reading reports of Sudan refugees in 1989. The Daily Telegraph featured a photo of a starving fourteen-year-old boy who died while the reporters were at the food camp. Many readers were moved to send money and the paper opened an appeal. Many readers sent letters with their cheques – a lot of them to the value of £14 – explaining that the amount was for each year of the teenager's life, and in that sense his death hadn't been in vain.

But when it comes to giving, money isn't everything. When Mother Theresa visited Britain a few years ago, she noted how people are treated and neglected in this country. She wondered at all the lonely people. And she declared, 'You, in Britain, have a different type of poverty.' Plenty of people *do* live in financial poverty in this country, but many others feel terribly alone. The richness we can offer is to be friends to these people. And God has a way of making much out of the little we give.

I was once waiting for a friend at London's Waterloo Station as we had tickets for a play at the National Theatre on the South Bank. Waterloo tends to attract society's fringe-dwellers, and while I was waiting I noticed a rough and drunken man trying to pull himself up from the stairs he was sitting on. He wasn't having much luck. It got to a point where I couldn't stand and watch any longer. I walked over to him and offered my hand and asked him if he wanted some help. He gladly took it and when he was standing said, 'You must be an angel.' I smiled, told him to look after himself and waved him 'good bye' and we parted on friendly terms. I came away from a simple human gesture with my heart warmed, and aware that it hadn't taken much to start to reach out to someone.

Maybe you've noticed that often less well-off people seem more generous than the wealthy. Going carol singing with the church youth club during my teens, I can still remember it striking me that it was the people in the big houses who gave the least, if at all – and on commenting to my mother, being told that that was why they had big houses . . .

Of course, that's not always true, but certainly money and what it can buy does have a power over people, and once they start amassing it, it's very difficult to shut off the desire for more. Indeed, many Christians are just as materialistic as their non-Christian neighbours. For 'whoever loves money never has money enough: whoever loves wealth is never satisfied with his income'.[6] Money takes a hold that cuts many off from seeing how others have to live.

Explains John Stott: 'We cannot maintain a "good

life" (of extravagance) and a "good conscience" simultaneously. One or other has to be sacrificed. Either we keep our conscience and reduce our affluence, or we keep our affluence and smother our conscience. We have to choose between God and mammon.'[7]

For it's not money that carries us through, though it helps. An enthusiasm for life and a love for Christ give us the strength and wisdom to use what little we have to further His cause, and to depend on Him rather than our bank balance to guide us across the world.

ACTION STATION

- Read:
  Pennies for Heaven: giving and Christian discipleship by Ian Coffey (Kingsway, 1984).
  Free is Cheaper by Ken Smith (John Ball, 1988).

- Give until it hurts. Give to the beggar, buy somebody a cup of tea or something to eat, and keep on doing it. Or send cheques to a range of organisations.

- Pray that God will give you what you need for your own personal use and to help you be more effective, and try and give the rest away.

- God loves a cheerful giver, and one that does it in secret too. Think of ways that you can help somebody and do it without them knowing. Similarly, do some environmental work for God without anybody else knowing what you're getting up to.

20

Praying for Change

So many things to pray about – the environment, animals, a Christian response, the Third World, the Western world's greed, a change in oneself . . . Just where do we start?

You can feel like Atlas taking the weight of the world's problems on your shoulders when you become concerned about the way we're treating God's planet and its people. So many things need doing, you can't help thinking that what you do to try and change things won't make much difference. Any practical moves you make seem worthless.

At the time of the 1986 Ethiopian famine I felt just that way. I'd seen the TV documentaries and David Bailey's photos and wept. I wrote off to various relief organisations like Oxfam and the World Development Movement to learn more. Caught up in the Geldof mood that swept the nation, I donated money, did a sponsored run and went to a big rock concert. I genned up on the issues and learnt about how the way we live here affects the way people live on the other side of the world, but all this still wasn't enough.

I felt frustrated and sad that it seemed I couldn't really make a great deal of difference. Governments, Big Business, the World Bank had the power and didn't really want to change. I cried out to God. And God heard my cry. Two years later He had me working for Tear Fund, the Christian Third World relief and development agency. Before I got the job I remember saying to my sister, 'If I get it, it'll be like coming home.'

Certainly we can get weighed down by what we feel

we can't do. But as Christians, it's up to us to hand the burden over to Jesus who after all took the mighty weight of our sins upon His shoulders.

'Come to me, all you who are weary and burdened, and I will give you rest. Take my yoke upon you and learn from me, for I am gentle and humble in heart, and you will find rest for your souls. For my yoke is easy and my burden is light.'[1]

By sharing the load with Him through prayer we become more unwilling to give up the fight for justice and truth. And we're assured of our value as individuals in His eyes and more prepared to make a stand, even on our own – though backed by Him – for what we believe in.

Prayer process
But it's still helpful to know how to go about praying for environmental issues. Think back to how you prayed when you first started getting interested in God's wider world. And start from there.

The first prayer I can ever remember praying was basically a roll call of the family, and I rattled it off every night for years. As I got a bit more confident in my faith, I started adding bits. I worried about pandas and all those animals on the brink of extinction, and what about all those creatures that to us seem rather gruesome but which God must like? I prayed 'for all the animals in the world'. And the other parts of God's creation – the trees, the seas and even the stones – 'for everything of nature'.

Young Nicki Mackenzie, who wrote a prayer which was published in Tear Fund's *Tearaways* magazine,[2] realises the extent of God's world, His power and His love: 'Dear Lord God, you made everything in creation from the smallest blade of grass to the whole galaxy: from the tiniest ant to the largest elephant or whale. You can create or destroy anything in the blink of an eyelid. Thank you for always being with us although we can never really show how much we do love you.'

Through such prayer, we come to recognise God's love through sensing the wonder of His creation. Find a stone, a gnarled piece of wood, a twig, in fact anything natural. Feel it, smell it, look closely at it, and use it as a way to direct your thoughts to God. Does this object tell of new life, of the way God smooths off our awkward parts, of His gentleness and strength? It's not that very different from Blake's impressions:

> To see a world in a Grain of Sand,
> And a Heaven in a Wild Flower,
> Hold Infinity in the palm of your hand,
> And Eternity in an hour.

And it helps us understand why we should do as much as we can to stop the destruction.

Spreading wings of prayer
As you learn more about God's world and He opens your eyes and your heart to how He feels about the way it's being treated, you begin to gain confidence in saying what you really feel when you pray. And the range of things we need to pray for becomes clear.

Be bold. The first time I ever joined a prayer group, I was at the time involved with the animal rights movement and keen on current affairs and part of my degree included Environmental Studies. I wanted to pray for the world.

But I wasn't used to praying aloud. As I sat in this circle of Christians with my eyes tightly closed I found myself getting increasingly frustrated and feeling more and more 'out of it' as everyone else seemed to be homing in on prayers for their next-door neighbour, problems with studying, that sort of thing. It now seems to me that that prayer group needed a good dose of prayer beyond domestic interests. I just didn't have the confidence to help push it that way.

There are a variety of Christian and non-Christian resources that you can use to help you pray. Keep up-to-date with environmental concerns by reading a newspaper regularly. Most papers now have a 'Green' or environmental column. As your interest grows, you'll find that some issues and parts of the world interest you more than others. Develop these interests so that your prayers are focused and informed.

If you belong to an environmental group such as Friends of the Earth or Greenpeace, or are on the mailing list of a charity like Oxfam or Tear Fund, use the material they send you as a starting point for prayer. Tear Fund has its own Prayer Diary as most Christian organisations do, and although this doesn't concentrate only on environmental matters, its coverage of Third World nations and projects Tear Fund supports is helpful. Some Christian books like the colourful and thought-provoking *Leaves from the Tree of Peace*[3] encourage prayer on a particular Green topic, and a specifically environmental prayer letter is available from Christian Ecology Link.

Prayer moves

As we draw ever closer to God, we find that our prayer life increasingly refuses to be boxed into nice neat sections of the day that we can deal with and then go on our merry way. Praying becomes far easier, and you can find yourself praying wherever you happen to be.

Soon after his conversion, Cliff Richard declared, 'It's

179

looking through Christian eyes that makes the difference.'
God opens our eyes to the world around us and the hurts
and joys of the community in which we live. Praying is
simply talking to God and we do that more and more
as His values become ours too.

'Every moment of life is holy,' states Vance Hays in
the youth-orientated book *The Time of Your Life*. 'Time
is God's gift, given so His creatures may glorify him.
Work, play and study can all be spiritual activities, given
over to praising the Lord. When Christians commit
themselves this way, their lives take on the quality of
holiness.

'Just as the workaholic shows by his lifestyle that he
has consecrated himself to his job, and many physical
fitness buffs adhere religiously to their early morning run,
Christians also show their commitments by the way they
live.'[4]

Prayer isn't just about kneeling and fixing our eyes
heavenward. It is done when we're busy getting our hands
dirty too. After hearing of the death of His cousin John
the Baptist, Jesus needed to be alone to grieve and be
with His Father. It's very interesting to learn that He
never stopped looking beyond Himself: 'When Jesus
heard what had happened, he withdrew by boat privately
to a solitary place. Hearing of this, the crowds followed
him on foot from the towns. When Jesus landed and saw
a large crowd, he had compassion on them and healed
their sick.'[5]

Jesus' bereavement – and with it the thoughts and
prayers of a recently bereaved person — were in a sense
put to one side. Yet at the same time his sorrow was
turned outward and into compassion for the crowds.
Jesus didn't stop praying. His very act of love and healing
shows up the continuance of the spiritual life through all
we do. If we are motivated by God to do something, if
we look to Him at all times so that our actions follow
through, then our lives become an act of prayer whether

we are silent and on our knees in a quiet place or cleaning out a river so that wildlife can thrive again.

Prayaway

Sometimes, like Greta Garbo, we just feel that we 'vant to be alone'. Most people shut their bedroom door and pray or visit an empty church where the atmosphere helps their mind home in on God. And this is certainly Christian: 'But when you pray, go into your room, close the door and pray to your Father, who is unseen. Then your Father, who sees what is done in secret, will reward you.'[6]

Yet prayer can be just as enriching — and secret — in a wide open space where there's nobody about for miles. When I find life getting too stressful and I need space to get close to God, the image that comes into my head is a quiet cliff top near a seaside town where I can sit on the grass and chat with God. If you live near the sea, then take a stroll along the beach and look out far over the water. You'll feel tiny, but be struck too by the awesome power of the sea — and God's might.

If you live in a city, then try and climb as high as possible whether on a natural hill-top or to the top of a building to catch a panoramic view. Tony Campolo remarks in *Who Switched the Price Tags*? of a moment when at the top of the Empire State Building on a school visit, he suddenly stopped charging around with his friends and just looked at the view. 'Then mystically, I took it all in — I experienced the city with an over-powering awareness. I stepped outside of myself and watched myself living and experiencing New York. I sucked in the scene.'[7] Basically he was awestruck. And if we open our eyes to our environment, there are plenty of times when we can be, too, and can lift such moments to God.

If we are prepared to pray in the middle of nowhere, then it's important that we pray *for* such places as well.

Going Green

The wilderness areas of the world like deserts and oceans are part of God's creation, and by praying for them we are snatching them out of the hands of the Devil. The wilderness was a special place where Jesus prayed. Alone in the desert and tempted by the Devil, He proved himself strong enough not to succumb,[8] and after being ministered to by angels, was able to return to society built up and ready for action.

The world's wilderness regions are special places where people can feel very close to God and aware of their limitations. Scientists in the Antarctic return from their research with stirring photographs of the frozen wastes, their hearts touched in a very artistic way by their surroundings.

Left behind on a rocky mountainside in Finse, southern Norway, I felt very frightened when the clouds came down and it started to rain. All I could do was pray and grip onto Jesus' hand. He gave me a tremendous sense of peace. I knew in one moment that if I were patient and didn't panic the clouds would lift and I'd be able to see my way down – and at exactly the same time I knew that it didn't matter if the clouds didn't lift. I was completely in Jesus' care, forever.

Wherever we are, we can use the moment for God. The community in which we live, the environment where we find ourselves, give us lots of pointers to help us get close to Him. Indeed, Beverley Parkin's gloriously illustrated *Flowers of the Wayside*[9] is like a seed catalogue of wild flowers reflecting different facets of God's love. The wonders of God's creation act as signposts heavenwards, giving us a glimpse of His wonder.

And knowing this should make us all the more determined to protect His planet. Our prayer takes on a new edge as God prompts us to pray for an end to the damage being done, and spurs us into action. Our Christian faith and the actions that stem from our being Christians are one and the same.

ACTION STATION

- Read:
  Out of the Deep: prayer as protest by Gordon
  Mursell (Darton, Longman & Todd, 1989).

- Find an old notebook or out-of-date diary, and
  under the different days of the week list people,
  places and issues that you want to pray for. And
  pray accordingly.

- Find a place close to home where you can be
  alone to pray among the wild life: a river bank,
  a piece of wasteland, a wooded area, an old tree.
  Make this a regular spot for time with God and
  His world.

- Pray that God will show you what He wants
  doing as you walk down the street. Ask Him to
  give you the strength to do His will.

Notes

Chapter 1. Introduction
1. E.F Schumacher, *Small is Beautiful*, Abacus, 1974.
2. Tom Sine, *The Mustard Seed Conspiracy: You can make a difference in tomorrow's troubled world*, Marc Europe, 1981, p.294–295.
3. Tony Campolo, *Who Switched the Price Tags: A search for values in a mixed-up world*, Word, 1987, p.48.
4. Tony Campolo, as above, p.40.
5. Andy Mayer and John Becker, *Zero Calorie Desserts*, Angus & Robertson, 1988.

Chapter 2. Green Christians — Off Colour?
1. *Daily Mail*, 8 June 1990.
2. Genesis 1: 1, 26, 31.
3. The Rt Rev Robert Wiliamson, Bishop of Bradford, *Church Times*, 9 June 1989, p.2.
4. *Christian News World*, June 1990, p.6.
5. *CEN*, 22 June 1990, p.6.
6. *CEN*, 22 June 1990, p.6.
7. John Stott, *Issues Facing Christians Today*, Marshalls, 1984, p.115.

Chapter 3. A Different Way of Seeing Green
1. Mark 14: 34–36.
2. Mark 5: 1–13.
3. Matthew 10: 39.
4. Matthew 6: 28–30.
5. Matthew 6: 26.
6. Genesis 2: 1.
7. Tear Fund, *Broken Image*, 1989.
8. Genesis 3: 17.

9. Isaiah 11: 6–9.
10. Romans 8: 8.
11. Romans 8: 19–24.

Chapter 4. Home Service
1. Matthew 8: 20.
2. Matthew 10: 5–15.
3. Matthew 6: 19–21.

Chapter 5. Food for Thought
1. 1 Corinthians 6: 19.
2. Matthew 4: 4.
3. Richard Mahey, *Food for Free*, Collins, 1989.
4. Genesis 1: 29–30.
5. Genesis 9: 1–3.
6. Janet Hunt, *A Vegetarian in the Family: Meatless recipes for the odd one out*, Thorsons, 1977.

Chapter 6. Dress Sense
1. Luke 12: 27–28.
2. Jonathon Holliman, *Consumer's Guide to the Protection of the Environment*, Pan/Ballantine, 1971.
3. Ronald Sider, *Rich Christians in an Age of Hunger*, Hodder & Stoughton, 1977.
4. Ruth Herring and Karen Manners *Knitting Wildlife*, Pavilion, 1989.
5. Matthew 5: 10.
6. Luke 3: 11.
7. Matthew 6: 1–4.

Chapter 7. Consuming Passions
1. Matthew 16: 36.
2. *New Consumer*, 52 Elswick Road, Newcastle upon Tyne NE4 6JH. Subscription: £12.00 per year for four issues
3. *Ethical Consumer*, ECRA Publishing Ltd, 100 Gretney Walk, Moss Side, Manchester M15 5ND. Subscription: £10.50 per year for six bi-monthly issues.

Chapter 8. Garden Party
1. John 15: 1–2.
2. Genesis 2: 15.
3. Richard Spurgeon, *Ecology*, Usbourne Science and Experiments, p.36–37.
4. Send an A4 envelope with a 50p stamp to Pondwatch, The Wildfowl and Wetlands Trust, Slimbridge, Glos GL2 7BT.
5. Richard Spurgeon, as above, p.5.
6. Genesis 3: 17–19.

Chapter 9. School of Thought
1. *The New Road*, World Wide Fund for Nature.

Chapter 10. Full Employment
1. *Jobs Abroad*, available for £1.65 from Christian Service Centre, Holloway Street, West Lower Gonal, Dudley, West Midlands.
2. *Careforce* – jointly sponsored by Scripture Union, UCCF, CYFA and Crusaders. Details from 130 City Road, London EC1V 2NJ.
3. Community Service Volunteers work on projects such as helping disabled people live at home, working in adventure playgrounds, psychiatric hospitals, night shelters and hostels. Contact CSV, 237 Pentonville Road, London N1 9NJ.
4. 'My Generation', *21CC*, July 1990, Elm House.

Chapter 11. Church Base
1. Andrew Linzey, 'And Every Living Creature That Moveth', *Church Times* 22 June 1990, p.8.
2. John Biggs, *Psalms For Today*, Baptist Times, 1989; and *Stewardship of the Soil* Baptist Men's Movement, 1989.
3. John 14: 6.

Chapter 12. Travelling Light
1. Mark 5: 25–34.
2. Matthew 21: 7.
3. Karen Christensen, *Home Ecology*, Arlington, 1989, p.125.
4. London Cycling Campaign/Kensington & Chelsea FoE, *On*

Your Bike, 1982 (latest edition by London Cycling Campaign, 1989).

5. Tom Isitt, 'Go Green' in *Motorbike International*, September 1989, Advanced Publishing, p.49.
6. Tom Isitt, as above, p.54.
7. Jonathon Holliman, *Consumer's Guide to the Protection of the Environment*. Pan/Ballantine, 1971, p.127.
8. Gary Numan, *Cars*, Beggars Banquet, 1980.
9. Greenpeace, *The Greenhouse Effect/The Greenpeace Solution*.
10. Jonathon Holliman, as above, p.40.
11. *New Consumer*, Autumn 1989. p.26.
12. Evangelical Alliance, *IDEA*, July 1990, p.13.
13. Friends of the Earth, *Help Save London from Massive Road Building*, FoE, 1990.

Chapter 14. Away From It All?
1. David Woodworth, *International Directory of Voluntary Work*, Vacation Work, 9 Park End Street, Oxford, £8.95.

Chapter 15. People In Green houses . . .
1. *Root and Branch*. Contact the CEL Local Groups Coordinator, c/o Joan Hart, 17 Burns Garden, Lincoln LN2 4LJ.
2. *Green Christians*. Write to CEL Secretary, Joan Hart, at the above address for further information about the CEL and to be put on the Green Christians mailing list.
3. Tim Cooper, 'Attacks on 'New Age' could discourage care of creation'. Press release from Christian Ecology Link, 21 August 1990.
4. Sheena Brown, letter to the author 11 June 1990.
5. *EAR*! Available with an introductory Earth Action Pack from Earth Action, 28 Underwood Street, London N1 7JQ.

Chapter 16. The Sky's the Limit
1. Matthew 8: 27.
2. Genesis 9: 13–15.

Chapter 17. Hands Across the Ocean
1. *New Internationalist*, 42 Hythe Bridge Street, Oxford OX1 2EP.
2. Isaiah 49: 15.
3. Bruce Brander, *Ethiopia: Five years later*, World Vision, 1989.

Chapter 18. Whose World Is It Anyway?
1. Edward Echlin, *The Christian Green Heritage: World as creation*, Grove Ethical Studies no. 74, Grove, 1989, p.6.
2. Sir Fred Catherwood, *God's Time, God's Money: Using time, talents and money efficiently*, Hodder & Stoughton, 1987, p.180.
3. William Kolzwinkle, *Doctor Rat*, A. Ellis, 1976.
4. Chris Eaton, 'Discovering', *Now You See Me, Now You Don't*, Cliff Richard, EMI, 1981.

Chapter 19. The Offering
1. Sir Fred Catherwood, *God's Time, God's Money: Using time, talents and money efficiently*, Hodder & Stoughton, 1987. p.180.
2. Sir Fred Catherwood, as above, p.181.
3. Luke 10: 30–37.
4. Matthew 25: 14–30.
5. Tony Campolo, *Who Switched the Price Tags: A search for values in a mixed-up world*, Word, 1987, p.14.
6. Ecclesiastes 5: 10.
7. John Stott, *Issues Facing Christians Today: A major appraisal of contemporary social and moral questions*, Marshalls, 1984, p.226.

Chapter 20. Praying for Change
1. Matthew 11: 28–30.
2. Nicki's Prayer, *Tearaways* No 24, 1989, Tear Fund, p.8.
3. John Reardon, ed. *Leaves from the Tree of Peace: A resource book of words and pictures*, United Reformed Church, 1986.

Notes

4. Vance Hays in *The Time of Your Life*, Macdonald, Campolo et al, Frameworks for Living, IVP, 1989, p.55–56.
5. Matthew 14: 13–14.
6. Matthew 6: 6.
7. Tony Campolo, *Who Switched the Price Tags: A search for values in a mixed-up world*, Word, 1987, p.41.
8. Matthew 4: 1–11.
9. Beverley Parkin, *Flowers of the Wayside*, Lion, 1989.

Organisations
to Contact

All the organisations listed below have featured in this book. They're Christian and non-Christian, and cover most Green and environmental issues. They are listed under the issue they represent. Write to them for further details, and it will save them some of their much-needed funds if you enclose an A4 stamped addressed envelope with your letter.

General Environmental Groups
Christian Ecology Link Joan Hart, 17 Burns Gardens, Lincoln, Lincs LN2 4LJ.
Friends of the Earth (and *Earth Action*) 26–28 Underwood Street, London N1 7JQ.
Greenpeace 36 Graham Street, London N1 8LL.

Animals
Animal Christian Concern 46 St Margarets Road, Horsforth, Leeds, West Yorkshire LS18 5BG.
British Union for the Aboliton of Vivisection 16A Crane Grove, London N7 8LB.
Compassion in World Farming (and *Farm Animal Rangers*) 20 Lavant Street, Petersfield GU32 3EW.
Lynx PO Box 509, Dunmow, Essex CM6 1UH.
RSPCA (and *Junior RSPCA*) Causeway, Horsham, West Sussex RH12 1HG.
Vegetarian Society (and *Scream Campaign*) Parkdale, Dunham Road, Altrincham, Cheshire WA14 4QG.

Habitat
British Trust for Conservation Volunteers 36 St Mary's Street, Wallingford, Oxon OX10 OEU.

Organisations to Contact

National Trust 36 Queen Anne's Gate, London SW1H 9AS.

Human Rights
Amnesty International 5 Roberts Place, London EX1R OEJ.
Jubilee Campaign PO Box 80, Cobham, Surrey KT11 2BQ.

Political Groups
Christian Democratic Forum c/o David Alton MP or Ken
  Hargreaves MP, House of Commons, London SW1A OAA.
Christian Ecology Link See under General Environmental
  Groups.
Christian Socialist Movement The Rev. Eric Wright, 36 Cross
  Flats Avenue, Leeds LS11 7BG.
Conservative Family Campaign Mrs Joan Pilgrem, April
  Cottage, 2 Long Fore, Godalming, Surrey GU7 3TD.
Green Party 10 Station Parade, Balham High Road, London
  SW12 9AZ.
Liberal Democrats Christian Forum Margaret Ferguson,
  Heather Hill, Southampton Road, Lyndhurst, Sussex SO34
  7BQ.
SDP Christian Forum Noel Ruttle, 29 Endcliffe Glen Road,
  Sheffield S11 8RW.

Third World
Christian Aid PO Box 100, London SE1 7RT.
Oxfam 274 Banbury Road, Oxford OX2 7DZ.
TEAR Fund 100 Church Road, Teddington, Middlesex TW11
  8QE.
Traidcraft Kingsway, Gateshead, Tyne and Wear NE11 ONE.
Voluntary Service Overseas 9 Belgrave Square, London SW1X
  8PW.
World Development Movement (WDM) Bedford Chambers,
  Covent Garden, London WC2E 8HA.
World Vision Dychurch House, 8 Abington Street,
  Northampton NN1 2AJ.

Wildlife
London Wildlife Trust Freepost, London N1 9BR.

RSPB (and *Young Ornithologists*) The Lodge, Sandy, Bedfordshire SG19 2DL.

Watch The Green, Witham Park, Lincoln LN5 7JR.

Wildfowl and Wetland Trust Slimbridge, Glos GL2 7BT.

World Wide Fund for Nature Panda House, Godalming, Surrey.

Youth Groups

Earth Action See under *Friends of the Earth* in the General Environmental Groups section.

Farm Animal Rangers See under *Compassion in World Farming* in the Animals section.

Girl Guides Association Commonwealth Headquarters, 17 Buckingham Palace Road, London SW1W OTT.

Junior RSPCA See under *RSPCA* in the Animals section.

Scout Association Baden-Powell House, 65 Queen's Gate, London SW7 5JS.

Scream Campaign See under *Vegetarian Society* in the Animals section.

Watch See Wildlife section.

Young Ornithologists See under *RSPB* in the Wildlife section.

Of course there are plenty of other organisations that are involved in Green activities. Your local library should have a copy of *Voluntary Agencies*, an annual directory published by Bedford Square which should be able to help you track down further relevant organisations.